WRITERS AND THEIR WORK

ISOBEL ARMSTRONG
General Editor

GERARD MANLEY HOPKINS

GERARD MANLEY HOPKINS

From a portrait of 1859, by Anne Eleanor Hopkins.

GERARD MANLEY HOPKINS

Daniel Brown

NORTHCOTE

BRITISH COUNCIL

ATLANTIC
PUBLISHERS & DISTRIBUTORS (P) LTD

This edition is published by

ATLANTIC

PUBLISHERS & DISTRIBUTORS (P) LTD

7/22, Ansari Road, Darya Ganj, New Delhi-110 002
Tel: 40775252, 23273880, 23275880, 23280451; Fax: +91-11-23285873
E-mail: orders@atlanticbooks.com; Web: www.atlanticbooks.com

By arrangement with
Northcote House Publishers Ltd
Horndon House, Horndon, Tavistock, Devon, PL19 9NQ,
United Kingdom. (T)+44(0)1822 810066; (F)+44(0)1822 810034
(E) northcote.house@virgin.net and (W) www.northcotehouse.co.uk
The *Writers and their Work* series is published in association with the British Council.

First Indian Reprint 2010
First published in 2004 by Northcote House Publishers Ltd

ISBN 978-81-269-1287-2

British Library Cataloguing-in-Publication Data
A catalogue record for this book is available from the British Library

Typeset by TW Typesetting, Plymouth, Devon
Printed in India at Nice Printing Press, A-33/3A, Site-IV,
Industrial Area, Sahibabad, Ghaziabad, U.P.

For Hilary Fraser,
and Fiona MacLean

Contents

Biographical Outline

1844	28 July: born in Stratford, Essex.
1852	Family moves to Oak Hill, Hampstead, where Hopkins is placed in a day school.
1854–62	At Highgate Grammar School, as a boarder. Wins several academic prizes, and a poetry prize for *The Escorial* (1860).
1863–7	At Balliol College, Oxford, where he graduated with a First in *Literae Humaniores* or 'Greats', which at the time was mainly a Classics and Philosophy course. His teachers included Benjamin Jowett, T. H. Green, and Walter Pater. He also made friends at Oxford with Robert Bridges, William Addis, E. H. Coleridge, and A. W. Mowbray Baillie.
1866	July: decides to convert to Roman Catholicism, and is received into the Church by J. H. Newman on 21 October.
1867	September to April 1868: teaches at Newman's Birmingham Oratory School.
1868	Writes his 'Parmenides' notes, which contain the first usages and explanations of his coinages 'instress' and 'inscape'. May: decides to become a priest; burns copies of early verses. July: hiking in the Swiss Alps with his friend Edward Bond, where they meet the physicist John Tyndall. September: enters the Jesuit Novitiate at Manresa House, Roehampton, London.
1870	September: studies Philosophy at St Mary's Hall, Stonyhurst.
1873	September: Professor of Rhetoric at Manresa House.

1874	September until October 1877: studies theology at St Beuno's College, North Wales.
1875	December to January 1876: writes 'The Wreck of the *Deutschland*'.
1877	February to September: a very productive period for his poetry writing. Poems from this time include 'God's Grandeur', 'As kingfishers catch fire', 'Spring', 'The Windhover', 'Pied Beauty', and 'Hurrahing in Harvest'. September: ordained as a priest. From October: teaching and parish work at Mount St Mary's College, Chesterfield.
1878	April to July: teaching undergraduates at Stonyhurst College, Lancashire. Wrote 'The Loss of the *Eurydice*'. July to November: acting Special Preacher at Farm Street Church, London. December to October 1879: curate at St Aloysius' Church, Oxford.
1879	Poems from this year include 'Duns Scotus' Oxford', 'Binsey Poplars', 'Henry Purcell', 'The Handsome Heart', and 'Andromeda'. October to December: curate at St Joseph's Church, Bedford Leigh, near Manchester. 30 December until August 1881: priest at St Francis Xavier's, Liverpool.
1880	Writes 'Felix Randal' and 'Spring and Fall'.
1881	August to October: a priest at St Joseph's, Glasgow. October to August 1882: tertianship at Roehampton.
1882	August to February 1884: teaching Classics at Stonyhurst College.
1884	February to his death in June 1889: Fellow of Classics and Professor of Greek and Latin Literature at University College Dublin.
1885	May: many of the 'sonnets of desolation' were probably written at this time, as was 'To what serves Mortal Beauty?'
1888	Writes 'That Nature is a Heraclitean Fire and of the comfort of the Resurrection'.
1889	8 June: dies of typhoid fever and is buried at Glasnevin Cemetary, Dublin.

Abbreviations and References

J. *The Journals and Papers of Gerard Manley Hopkins*, ed. Humphry House and Graham Storey (London: Oxford University Press, 1959)

JP *Journals and Papers of Gerard Manley Hopkins*, ed. Giuseppe Castorina (Bari: Adriatica, 1974)

L1 *The Letters of Gerard Manley Hopkins to Robert Bridges*, ed. Claude Colleer Abbott, 2nd (rev.) impression (London: Oxford University Press, 1955)

L2 *The Correspondence of Gerard Manley Hopkins and Richard Watson Dixon*, ed. Claude Colleer Abbott, 2nd (rev.) impression (London: Oxford University Press, 1955)

L3 *Further Letters of Gerard Manley Hopkins*, ed. Claude Colleer Abbott, 2nd edn. (London: Oxford University Press, 1956)

P. *The Poems of Gerard Manley Hopkins*, ed. W. H. Gardner and N. H. MacKenzie, 4th (rev.) edn. (Oxford: Oxford University Press, 1970). References are to poem numbers

PM *The Early Poetic Manuscripts and Note-books of Gerard Manley Hopkins in Facsimile*, ed. Norman H. MacKenzie (New York: Garland, 1989)

PW *The Poetical Works of Gerard Manley Hopkins*, ed. Norman H. MacKenzie (Oxford: Clarendon Press, 1990). Unless otherwise indicated, references are to poem numbers

S. *The Sermons and Devotional Writings of Gerard Manley Hopkins*, ed. Christopher Devlin (London: Oxford University Press, 1959)

1

Eccentricity

Even as a young man, Gerard Manley Hopkins was criticized for writing unconventional poetry. In a letter from 1867, when he was 22, his friend E. W. Urquhart takes issue with one of his poems on the grounds that 'Too many licences are taken for a beginner.' Hopkins responds confidently to this charge by sketching a history of art in which the work of canonical artists is categorized by its eccentricities: 'I think you w[oul]d find in the history of Art that licences and eccentricities are to [be] found fully as often in beginners as in those who have established themselves and can afford them; those in Milton, Turner, and Beethoven are at the end, those in Shakspere, Keats, Millais, and Tennyson at the beginning' (*L3* 36). The licences that Urquhart criticizes him for are, Hopkins suggests, consistent with future greatness. Canonical art is appreciated here not for embodying conservative values of coherence and continuity but for being divergent and innovative.

From an early age Hopkins regarded singularity in art as normal and necessary. The rationale for this attitude is his belief that, as he writes to his friend and fellow poet Coventry Patmore in 1886, 'every true poet . . . must be original and originality a condition of poetic genius; so that each poet is like a species in nature (*not* an *individuum genericum* or *specificum*) and can never recur' (*L3* 370). Poetry is for Hopkins the exercise and fulfilment of the poet's distinctive nature, which makes him 'like a species in nature'. He follows Aristotle in thinking of the human soul and species in nature each as a latent form, a potential that is actualized in the life of the creature. Such form is realized through activity, which, as Hopkins's poem 'As kingfishers catch fire' makes clear, accordingly defines and expresses the creature's nature and purpose: '*What I do is me: for that I came*' (*P.* 57). This expressivist doctrine naturalizes the idea of the individual 'poetic genius' that Hopkins identifies with 'every true poet' and sanctions the full development and expression of such 'originality'. It gives Hopkins full licence to develop qualities that most clearly distinguish him from other poets and indeed from other people generally – to express himself in poetry that may strike others as odd or eccentric.

The question of how to read Hopkins's individualistic poetry arose with its earliest readers, his friends Robert Bridges, Coventry Patmore, and Richard Watson Dixon, and it has consistently preoccupied critics and readers since the posthumous publication of his *Poems* in 1918, almost thirty years after his death. By exploring the implications that this issue had both for the poet himself and for Hopkins studies as they emerged during the first half of the twentieth century, the present chapter aims to clear a path for its reading of a poet whose reputation for 'difficulty' and 'eccentricity' still precedes him.

Convinced of the uniqueness of each creative artist, which as he writes 'can never recur', Hopkins urged his fellow poets and friends Bridges, Patmore, and Dixon to publish their works and hoped that their readership would grow. Of Hopkins's work, however, only a few minor poems were published during his lifetime, while his only abiding readership was a private one, consisting of his three friends. He submitted 'The Wreck of the *Deutschland*', the first of the mature poems by which he is best known, to the Jesuit journal the *Month* for July 1876, but it would remain unpublished until 1918. When he wrote this, his longest poem, and subsequent poems, which were not intended for publication, Hopkins did so unhindered by considerations of public taste and opinion. Nor did he allow his work to be constrained by his friends' criticisms, as he makes plain in a letter to Bridges: 'I cannot think of altering anything. Why sh[oul]d I? I do not write for the public. You are my public and I hope to convert you' (*L1* 46). Confident in his poetry here to the point of proselytizing, Hopkins is like William Blake, a rare type of artist who is able to sustain his art and maintain his creative coherence without public recognition.

The uncompromising nature of Hopkins's poetry and the dignified defences of it he offers to Bridges and his other friends indicate a strongly independent character. He describes his intense sense of selfhood in some theological notes from 1880: 'Nothing else in nature comes near this unspeakable stress of pitch, distinctiveness, and selving, this selfbeing of my own.' This sense of self is, he writes, 'more distinctive than the taste of ale or alum, more distinctive than the smell of walnutleaf or camphor' (*S.* 123). While selfhood is experienced here as unique and autonomous, as original, it is also described as inexpressible and alienating, 'unspeakable'. Hopkins cherishes and cultivates his independence, a quality that leaves him vulnerable to feelings of isolation and loneliness. An unfinished poem from 1864, 'I am like a slip of comet', which may have been written as a speech for an unfinished play, *Floris in Italy* (*P.* 103), indicates Hopkins's early identification with an astronomical body that shines alone in the universe. By likening herself to a comet, the unnamed persona is indeed declaring her literal eccentricity, for she does not participate in the orderly eternal orbits around the sun that give 'the sistering planets' their relation to one another. An outsider from this system, the comet passes through space alone, drawing heat from the 'contagious sun' before it punningly 'goes out into the cavernous dark' and – 'So I go out' – dies. With the comet the young Hopkins creates a melancholy emblem for the life of independence and isolation that sums up much of his adult life.

Born on the 28 July 1844 to a middle-class Anglican family, Hopkins grew up in Hampstead, North London, and attended Highgate Grammar School, from 1854 to 1862, mainly as a boarder. His battles with the headmaster at Highgate indicate the young Hopkins's wilful independence: 'Dyne and I had a terrific altercation. I was driven out of patience and cheeked him wildly, and he blazed into me with his riding-whip' (*L3* 2). Writing to Arthur Hopkins in 1890, the year after Gerard's death, Hopkins's schoolfriend C. N. Luxmoore recalls such conflicts, which he says were the consequence of his friend's moral and intellectual integrity: 'If a fault be chargeable to your brother, it was the being unable to suffer wrong silently, the insisting on arguing his case with a man whose logic was comprised in the birch, to whom an answer however respectful was at least mutiny, if not rank blasphemy' (*L3* 396). From school he matriculated to university, becoming one of the first generation of middle-class students at Oxford. Hopkins studied Classics and Philosophy from April 1863 to June 1867 at Balliol, the most liberal and intellectually engaged of the Oxford colleges at this time. The Master of Balliol was Benjamin Jowett, the great Plato scholar and Germanist who was notorious for his contribution to the immensely controversial biblical critical volume, *Essays and Reviews* (1860).

Hopkins's freedom and independence of thought were encouraged by Jowett and other teachers, such as Walter Pater and the liberal moral philosopher T. H. Green, even though the direction it took him, towards Roman Catholicism, was not one that they encouraged or approved of. His anguish over his religious beliefs in 1865, as he contemplated leaving the Anglican Church, left him feeling rebuffed by the universe: 'My prayers must meet a brazen heaven | And fail or scatter all away' (*P.* 18). Other poems from this year, such as 'Where art thou friend, whom I shall never see' (*P.* 13), 'Myself unholy' (*P.* 16), and 'See how Spring opens with disabling cold' (*P.* 17), also indicate rather bleak and lonely states of mind. Hopkins set himself apart from his family and most of his peers at Oxford by joining the Catholic Church in October 1866, a position that became more entrenched when in May 1868 he decided to enter the priesthood. His status as a convert to Catholicism would mean that he was not always wholeheartedly accepted by his religious peers, especially during his time as Professor of Greek and Latin at the recently established University College Dublin, from 1884 to his death in 1889. This period of growing nationalist agitation around the figure of Parnell and his downfall was not a good time to be an English convert in Ireland. A Jesuit colleague in Dublin testifies to the treatment that Hopkins received and the extent of his alienation: 'Gerald Hopkins was at an opposite pole to every thing around him: literary, political, social &c. (a thorough John Bull incapable of understanding Rebel Ireland). No one took him seriously; he played the part rather of the droll jester, in the medieval castles.'[1] The writer demonstrates the sincerity of his views on Hopkins by not taking 'him seriously' enough to get his first name right.

Writing to Bridges in 1881 Hopkins observes that the charge of oddness had plagued him throughout his life and not just in relation to his poetry: 'You give me a long jobation about eccentricities. Alas, I have heard so much about and suffered so much for and in fact been so completely ruined for life by my alleged singularities that they are a sore subject' (*L1* 126). Unfettered by the prevailing conventions and tastes that would have made it more accessible to his contemporaries, Hopkins's poetry was often misunderstood and unappreciated by its small but valued readership. The deeply personal nature of his poetry, his heightened sense of it as clarifying and expressing a core selfhood, meant that there was a great deal at stake for him in writing it and in having his closest friends appreciate it. There is a sad irony in the fact that the very distinctiveness of Hopkins's poetry not only required sympathetic understanding but also served to frustrate such understanding, for Bridges, Patmore, and even Dixon, his most enthusiastic reader, found it quirky and difficult. Even so they evidently offered him sufficient support for him to write: 'There is', he writes in 1885, 'a point with me in matters of any size when I must absolutely have encouragement as much as crops rain; afterwards I am independent' (*L1* 218–19).

Hopkins appears to have experienced his artistic alienation, along with other feelings of personal isolation, most intensely during his last years in Dublin. This crisis is documented by the sequence of poems that are conventionally referred to as the 'dark' or 'terrible' sonnets, or the 'sonnets of desolation' (*P.* 64–9, 74). The first and second stanzas of the sonnet beginning 'To seem the stranger lies my lot' (*P.* 66), which dates probably from 1885, outline Hopkins's estrangement from his family and England, while the final tercets come to focus upon his frustrated will to express himself and be heard:

> I am in Ireland now; now I am at a third
> Remove. Not but in all removes I can
> Kind love both give and get. Only what word
>
> Wisest my heart breeds dark heaven's baffling ban
> Bars or hell's spell thwarts. This to hoard unheard,
> Heard unheeded, leaves me a lonely began.

Earlier in the poem England is described by the poet as 'wife | To my creating thought, [who] would neither hear | Me, were I pleading'. The final lines of the poem offer a curious parallel to this imagery of procreation, as the poet is feminized with a womblike heart that breeds a 'word | Wisest.' The phrase 'what word |Wisest my heart breeds' suggests the poet's fundamental creative act, that of choosing particular words and using them to generate new meanings. The words that his 'heart breeds' can be read as referring to his poems, which he describes as his children in 'To R. B.' (*P*. 76), as well as to the many coinages, such as 'instress' and 'inscape', he devises to express his most distinctive ideas and observations. More specifically, the 'word | Wisest' here indicates a reference to God or the *Logos*, the divine Word or Reason. It suggests that the words that the poet's 'heart breeds' are intended to acknowledge and honour God in the manner of the tall nun in 'The Wreck of the *Deutschland*', who, parallel to the Virgin Mary's actual pregancy, conceives of Christ in her mind and renews the incarnation of the Word made flesh by uttering his name: 'But here was heart-throe, birth of a brain, | Word, that heard and kept thee and uttered thee outright' (*P* 28, st. 30). In the later poem, however, the poet's words are inexplicably barred by heaven or thwarted by 'hell's spell'. Moreover, this is an experience that the poet has evidently had many times, for it is presented as a corollary of 'what word | Wisest' – that is, whatever word the poet's 'heart breeds'. Such experiences are cumulative, as the use of the verb 'to hoard' in the penultimate line makes clear, and each occurrence serves to reiterate the poet's diminished sense of himself: 'This to hoard unheard, | Heard unheeded, leaves me a lonely began.'

The word 'hoard' functions here not only as a verb but also as a noun, in the sense that 'This' – that is, each 'word | Wisest' – is relegated 'to [a] hoard unheard', a private store or treasury. Either way, that which is hoarded is a potential that has not been allowed to be realized, a type of arrested pregnancy. It can be understood as a potential that is either buried in the heart of the creator, unrealized and unexpressed, or realized but hidden away for the lack of a receptive audience; 'Heard unheeded', disregarded and uncared for. The personal hoard of work that Hopkins kept and that, largely thanks to Bridges, survived the period from his death in 1889 until his growing fame in the 1920s and 1930s led to their partial publication include his school notes on mechanics and mathematics, his Oxford and Birmingham essays and notes on philosophy and other subjects, his early notebooks and diaries, his sketch-books, his sermons and other religious writings, his poetry, and some of his musical settings. Another, latent, hoard is also suggested by the projects he embarked upon but did not finish, which include several verse dramas, musical compositions, papers on the subjects of Sacrifice, Aeschylus, Statistics and Free Will, and the Argei, and books on the Dorian Measure, Homer, and Light and the Ether. In an 1885 letter to his old friend Alexander Baillie Hopkins writes of his reluctance to destroy some of his remaining papers and reflects upon 'my old notebooks and beginnings of things, ever so many, which it seems to me might well have been done, ruins and wrecks' (*L3* 255).

In the final lines of 'To seem the stranger lies my lot', as is so often the case in Hopkins's poetry, meaning is enacted through vital relations between word sounds. The pattern of the word sounds 'hoard unheard, | Heard unheeded' is grounded in the positive meanings that the poem attaches to both the word 'hoard', which, as mentioned earlier, implies either a potential or an actual achievement, and the reciprocal principle, 'Heard', which implies both the expression and reception, the recognition, of such achievement. Both of these values are systematically negated in this sequence by the prefix added to the words that follow and echo each of them ('unheard . . . unheeded'), and more abstractly through the progressive thinning of their core vowel sounds, from the full sound of 'hoard', which gradually diminishes in 'heard', and the long and short *e*s of 'heeded'. This withering pattern undergirds and dramatizes the poet's sense of himself as undeveloped, deprived of the conditions by which his distinctive nature could flourish. It is a lack that, as he puts it, 'leaves me a lonely began'.

In Hopkins's early letter to Urquhart, where he discusses art and eccentricity, the category of 'beginners' gains its significance only in relation to the later achievement of the 'established' artists they develop into. A beginning implies subsequent progress and an ending; it is a relative term. The end of Hopkins's poem, indeed its very last word, describes a beginning that is arrested forever as the verb's past tense coagulates oddly into a noun, the sterile singularity of a 'began'. Here, it seems, is an example of a 'word' that Hopkins's distinctive 'heart breeds'. His odd usage renders the word a misfit, an outcast from the English language system, a parallel to the poet in his estrangement from England itself. An outlaw from accepted language usage, this freakish 'began' is itself alone, doomed to be 'lonely'. Indeed, its placement as the last word in the poem makes it literally preposterous. By representing himself with this final word, as merely a stalled start that pessimistically usurps the resolution and final achievement of an ending, Hopkins sees his singularity to end not in unique artistic and intellectual attainments, but personal loneliness and deep alienation and frustration. The curious phrase 'a lonely began' sums him up as a fruitless violation of convention. Hopkins personifies himself here in accordance with the common criticisms of his poetry as an example of eccentric or licentious language use.

Hopkins's reputation for eccentricity was evidently a great problem for him when he was alive, but it may also be seen as a problem for his readers after his death. This persistent reputation can stand in the way of later readers gaining a full and sympathetic understanding of his poetry, just as it did for his peers. The aptly named Bridges furnishes the link between the small private readership that Hopkins had during his lifetime and the large following his work gained in the twentieth century. Bridges edited the first edition of *Poems* in 1918, and it is through him that the reputation for oddness that Hopkins had in life also entered the public domain. Bridges' 'Preface to [the] Notes' for the first edition introduces Hopkins's work through its 'Oddity and Obscurity', apologetically anticipating (and indeed thereby establishing) criticisms of his friend's 'faults of taste' and 'blemishes in the poet's style'. Bridges evidently did not expect Hopkins's poetry to be well received and his commentary is understandably full of concessions to a readership that he thinks likely to dismiss it. In the 'Preface to [the] Notes', as in the earlier letters to Hopkins himself, Bridges approaches his friend's poetry from the premiss that there are established and authoritative critical norms against which it should be read and evaluated. Poet Laureate from 1913, Bridges addresses the 'Preface' to a conservative readership, whom he encourages to tolerate Hopkins's breaks with convention: 'there are definite faults of style which a reader must have courage to face, and must in some measure condone before he can discover the great beauties.'[2]

The period that separates the first edition in 1918 from the second in 1930 coincides with the high period of modernist poetry, an apt and receptive context for Hopkins's formal experimentation and innovations to be appreciated on their own terms. Indeed such modernist criteria were brought to readings of the poems during the 1920s and 1930s by such figures as J. Middleton Murry, Laura Riding and Robert Graves, I. A. Richards, William Empson, F. R. Leavis, Herbert Read, and Geoffrey Grigson.[3] Nevertheless, the discourse of Hopkins criticism was established and shaped decisively by Bridges' edition. Thus, for example, W. H. Gardner's pioneering two-volume study *Gerard Manley Hopkins: A Study of Poetic Idiosyncrasy in Relation to Poetic Tradition* (1944, 1949) accepts Bridges' premiss that Hopkins should be evaluated by the criteria of established norms in order to argue that his poems can in fact be integrated into the Western canon, that he 'is actually and eminently as legitimate an offspring of the great European poetic tradition as any English poet before him'.[4] For this reconciliation to occur, however, the author has, as the subtitle of the book demonstrates, to begin by presupposing the antithesis between 'Poetic Idiosyncrasy' and 'Poetic Tradition'.

The idea of a canon, of a coherent and continuous principle of 'Poetic Tradition' that Bridges and Gardner presuppose, marks the standard of 'High' art by which other works can be judged as lesser or 'Low' art. It defines the centre of culture, the norm, in relation to which texts that do not conform to its standards and conventions can be judged eccentric, abnormal. Hopkins partially collapses this distinction in his early letter to Urquhart, where eccentricity is identified with the mainstream of historical art practice, with canonical poets from Shakespeare to Tennyson. In an 1888 letter to Bridges, who has apparently suggested that he attend more closely to canonical works as models for his own poetry, Hopkins writes that on the contrary he is in the habit of defining his poetic practice *against* such works: 'The effect of studying masterpieces is to make me admire and do otherwise. So it must be on every original artist to some degree, on me to a marked degree. Perhaps then more reading would only *refine my singularity*, which is not what you want' (*L1* 291). Hopkins, the contemporary of Mallarmé and Whitman as well as of Bridges and Patmore, champions the proliferation of diverse and original artistic practices. He appreciates art through the principle of difference rather than, as Bridges does, conformity to criteria that he finds embodied by the canon. In this respect Hopkins's model of culture has a broad affinity with ways in which it is theorized in our own day.

Various strands of recent literary and cultural studies, such as postructuralism, gender studies and feminism, postcolonialism, new historicism, and readings grounded in considerations of class and race, have all served to question the dominant interests and perspectives that have formed and perpetuated the canon. Instead of the hierarchy of the canon, which categorizes creative work from 'High' down to 'Low' art, the tendency in our age is to see the full range of cultural phenomena to coexist on the same level as texts, without a definitive centre, each functioning on its own terms within the specific contexts of its production and reception. Even more than the era of modernist experimentation and individualism in which he gained his first public readership, our own age of postmodernism offers an apt and receptive climate in which to read Hopkins's work. In its recognition of diverse coexisting cultural phenomena postmodernism marks the final abandonment of the fixed criteria of tradition and the canon that Bridges and others brought to bear upon Hopkins's poetry. From an early age, indeed in 1863 when he was nineteen, Hopkins recognized the prevalence and danger of such prescriptive approaches to art, and championed the opposing principle of critical openness: 'The most inveterate fault of critics is the tendency to cramp and hedge in by rules the free movements of genius, so that I should say . . . the first requisite for a critic is liberality, and the second liberality, and the third, liberality' (*L3* 204).

Hopkins's critical 'liberality' maintains that the originality of each artist should be judged on its own terms, not by imposing prescriptive criteria from outside. Indeed, his work has to be approached literally on its own terms, for so much of its originality is registered in his coinages, such as 'inscape' and 'Sprung Rhythm'. He writes to Bridges of a book that he began writing on the Dorian Measure that 'It is full of new words, without which there can be no new science' (*L1* 254). Such coinages highlight the independence of his thought and the privacy in which he worked. Without having to make concessions to the tastes and understandings of a larger reading public, the body of work he produced developed, as we will see in the next chapter, according to its own internal motives and logic, so that it often strikes its readers as hermetic and inaccessible. This is another argument for introducing it on its own terms and as a whole, as a group of interrelated writings that work together to explain one another. The range of work that Hopkins preserved and so presumably valued throughout his life, including his prose writings on language, nature, philosophy, and theology, not only cast light on each other but elucidate the poetry in which many of their ideas are crystallized.

2

Concentricity

Hopkins's view of the canon is a decentred one in which the work and aesthetic style of each original artist radiates from – and so coheres around – its *own* centre, its own distinctive character and convictions. In an unfinished and untitled poem from early January 1866, selfhood is described as the inevitable centre from which the poet experiences the world: 'I am the midst of every zone|And justify the East and West' (*P.* 130). It is not eccentricity but rather concentricity that defines the poet's sense of himself here, for this vision of the world arranges itself about his 'all-accepting fixéd eye'. The poem, however, ends with a wish to escape from this fixed centralized selfhood: 'O lovely ease in change of place! | I have desired, desired to pass . . .'. In his commentary on this poem J. Hillis Miller observes that the poet's wish 'to pass beyond the situation of being always the center of the world'[1] is the key to a desire expressed in a poem written a few months earlier, in late October 1865, to be assimilated into another model of concentricity:

> Let me be to Thee as the circling bird,
> Or bat with tender and air-crisping wings
> That shapes in half-light his departing rings,
> From both of whom a changeless note is heard.
>
> (*P.* 19)

Hopkins figures his life and art in this poem as a pattern of concentric circles around the newly 'found . . . dominant of my range and state – | Love, O my God, to call Thee Love and Love'. The 'dominant' is not only a ruler or commanding authority, but a musical term for the fifth note of the scale of a key, which is especially important in defining harmonies. In other words this 'dominant', God or 'Love', draws the poet's being into harmony. The conceit around which 'Let me be to Thee' is organized derives from Pythagoreanism, a school of classical Greek philosophy that regards number as the eternal principle of order that determines the relations of musical harmony and the regular movements of the planets. It explains the latter with the doctrine of the harmony of the spheres, which theorizes the universe as a series of concentric spheres, each of which is studded with astronomical bodies and moves around their common centre at numerically fixed intervals.[2] The sounds that these concentric movements make are understood to harmonize with one another and so produce a celestial music. The imagery of Hopkins's poem draws upon both the geometrical and musical arrangement of the spheres and the harmony they generate. God is the geometrical centre that radiates, and the 'dominant' note that reverberates, outwards in the universe of the poem, just as the utterances and actions of 'the circling bird' and the bat move outwards from their 'changeless note' in the form of both resonant sound waves and their circling flight, which are punningly referred to here in the bat's 'departing rings'. Hopkins extends Pythagoreanism, which originally described planetary and other astronomical relations, to organic nature. The bird's and the bat's patterns of sound and flight enact a microcosmic version of the harmony of the spheres.

As Hopkins's poem demonstrates, Pythagoreanism lends itself to such efforts to describe the universe as theocentric, God-centred. The Pythagorean ideas of number and harmony are amongst the earliest principles of philosophical idealism, which argues against the common-sense view that identifies appearances (that which we see, hear, and otherwise perceive through the senses) with reality by asserting that, on the contrary, eternal thoughts or ideas are the ground of the world, the ultimate reality. By conceiving of the universe in terms of such unchanging ideas, the Pythagorean philosophy allows them to be identified with the mind of God. Pythagoreanism draws out the theological implications of idealism, for, if ideas do order the objective world, they would seem to require a source, an original thinker – namely, a creator God, the *Logos* or Reason. The *Logos* or Word that Hopkins nominates here as 'Love' is 'The authentic cadence'. A cadence is a point of rest or repose at the close of a musical phrase, a relaxation and resolution of musical movement or tension. It furnishes a metaphor for the resolution of his recent anguish over his religious belief and conversion, the rest or peace that closes this period. The authentic cadence is a chord progression from the dominant to the tonic, which most clearly defines its key. The 'authentic cadence' that the poet has taken to heart reciprocally reverberates outwards to draw his life and experience of the world into harmony: 'I have found my music in a common word.' Written a year before his formal conversion to Roman Catholicism, the poem strongly suggests that some version of this religion has superseded his Anglican faith:

> The authentic cadence was discovered late
> Which ends those only strains that I approve,
> And other science all gone out of date
> And minor sweetness scarce made mention of:
> I have found the dominant of my range and state –
> Love, O my God, to call Thee Love and Love.

The concentrically arranged cosmology that resonates from the 'changeless note' is identified with 'The authentic cadence', the true Church that accordingly renders other versions of Christianity redundant. Although they are not explicitly identified here, it is clearly Anglicanism that is referred to as 'out of date'. The title of the poem that immediately follows 'Let me be to Thee' in the manuscript of the early diaries describes the Anglican Church as 'The Half-way House' (*J.* 71; *P.* 20), a temporary residence for the poet on the way to his permanent home in the Catholic Church. A letter to Urquhart from September 1866 indicates that Hopkins had a sense of himself as becoming a Catholic at the time he wrote these poems: 'the silent conviction that I was to become a Catholic has been present to me for a year perhaps, as strongly, in spite of my resistance to it when it formed itself into words, as if I had already determined it' (*L3* 27). Another poem from a few months before 'Let me be to Thee', 'See how Spring opens with disabling cold' (*P.* 17), alludes to his process of conversion with regret at the time it has taken: 'Therefore how bitter, and learnt how late, the truth!' 'Let me be to Thee' is rather more positive in its construal of this process. 'The authentic cadence was discovered late', but as a 'cadence' it implies a musical sequence that preceded it, so that his earlier beliefs are described accordingly as musical 'strains' and his distress and agitation over them become part of a musical pattern that culminates in these last definitive notes of repose.

Hopkins's poem suggests that its Christian reworking of Pythagoreanism, in superseding 'other science', is itself a new 'science', a term that refers here to a logically systematic body of knowledge, which may be philosophical or theological, or indeed scientific in the conventional modern sense. In an 1866 letter to his father Hopkins explains that his new belief is based upon logical criteria, 'simple and strictly drawn arguments partly my own, partly others' (*L3* 93), while in a letter to Urquhart from the following year he refers to 'the Anglican logical break-down' (*L3* 48) that makes his earlier faith unsustainable, the 'other science all gone out of date'. In his letter to Urquhart from September 1866 he indicates that he was guided in his eventual conversion by an almost perverse independence from the influence and arguments of others: 'to see or hear "Romanising" things w[oul]d throw me back on the English Church as a rule' (*L3* 27). The tendency independently to theorize the grounds of his faith, to elaborate them as a science, a coherent system, remains with Hopkins throughout his life. Its most important expression comes, however, in 1868, in his 'Notes on the History of Greek Philosophy'. It is in these notes, written in the year after he finished his Oxford degree in Classics and Philosophy, that he formulates his metaphysic of 'instress' and 'inscape'. This doctrine describes Hopkins's conception of form in nature, the relation of such forms to God, and how we can know them. It follows the broad outlines of the 'science' sketched in 'Let me be to Thee' by elaborating a complete cosmology around its central principle of ultimate Being or God.

By articulating its desire and introducing the 'science' that it anticipates will fulfil it, 'Let me be to Thee as the circling bird' effectively announces a broad project that encompasses most of Hopkins's extant writings, and that most of the present book is dedicated to tracing. That he outlines this 'science' in terms of Pythagoreanism indicates the breadth and ambition of his conception. Pythagoreanism belongs to a time before the strict modern divisions between art, science, and philosophy were made. The Pythagoreans are attributed with being the first to recognize the mathematical basis of music. They are said to have done this by observing the direct ratio between the lengths of taut strings and the sound they make, a discovery that draws together our categories of art and science. This relation is of course amplifed in the doctrine of the harmony of the spheres, a cosmology that in the poem allows Hopkins to conceive of God as both loving and a rational principle that guarantees order and pattern in the universe. Pythagorean philosophy allows Hopkins to outline the relation he wishes to have to God and the world, a relation that fulfuls his whole being, for the understanding it allows of music integrates the rationality of mathematics and logical system with both emotional and aesthetic affect, the harmonious 'music' that, as he writes in 'Let me be to Thee', he prefers to 'each pleasurable throat that sings | And every praiséd sequence of sweet strings'.

As is clear from the opening words that give the poem its title, 'Let me be to Thee as the circling bird' expresses the poet's desire. It is a vision of the universe and his place in it that he hopes will be realized through his new faith, his new 'science'. Other poems from around the time this poem was written document feelings of alienation – prayers that 'fail or scatter all away' (*P*. 18), or, as in the untitled poem cited at the start of this chapter, the persona's sense of being closed off from the outside world by his solipsistic experience of it: 'The earth and heaven, so little known, | Are measured outwards from my breast' (*P*. 130). Hopkins's experience of the world clearly affronts and resists his hope that reality can be understood as a theocentric cosmology and that he can find a place within it. He accordingly has to work to establish this vision, which he does not only through his metaphysic of 'inscape', but throughout his writings on language, nature, theology, and poetry. An unfinished poem from July 1864 expresses his determination to face and overcome the discrepancy between his desire and his experience of the world:

I must hunt down the prize
  Where my heart lists.
Must see the eagle's bulk, render'd in mists,
  Hang of a treble size.

Must see the green seas roll
  Where waters set
Towards those wastes where the ice-blocks tilt and fret,
  Not so far from the pole.

(*P.* 88)

The 'prize' that is hunted in these Arctic wastes is the clear perception of form in nature, the goal of distinguishing the reality of 'the eagle's bulk' from its enlarged shadow 'render'd in mists'. The poem states a desire to find form in the heart of the most fluctuous natural phenomena, the extreme conditions of the Arctic where the seas alternate between states of liquidity and solidity. This is a determination that drives Hopkins's explorations of natural phenomena in the early diaries and journals: 'The shores are swimming and the eyes have before them a region of milky surf but it is hard for them to unpack the huddling and gnarls of the water and law out the shapes and the sequence of the running' (*J.* 223). In approaching nature in his early observations Hopkins assumes that each phenomenon has a defining law that can be brought out. It is, however, a form that is often obscured by the density of detail it presents to the eye, so that it needs to be 'unpack[ed]', its parts distinguished and the relations between them identified. The task that the persona of the poem sets himself to 'hunt down the prize' can be understood as a metaphor for his early efforts to 'law out' natural phenomena, to discover its defining forms.

'I must hunt down the prize' is the unfinished companion poem to the better known 'Heaven-Haven: A nun takes the veil' (*P.* 9), which presents a quite different attitude to nature from that of comprehension and conquest. The persona of this poem expresses a wish to avoid certain natural phenomena, many of which are milder manifestations of those that the Arctic explorer in the other poem confronts:

I have desired to go
  Where springs not fail,
To fields where flies no sharp and sided hail . . .

She has 'asked to be | Where no storms come' and 'out of the swing of the sea'. Most of the nun's wishes are cast in the negative. She requests a subdued and stable nature, in which the dynamism that so fascinates Hopkins in the journals and later poems is suppressed; there are no storms and the tides are muzzled, 'the green swell is in the havens dumb'. Here indeed, as the subtitle of the poem puts it, 'A nun takes the veil'; she assumes the religious life as a protective veneer against the real world of natural flux. This nun, the antithesis of the tall nun who heroically faces the fatal storm at sea in 'The Wreck of the *Deutschland*', is not a persona that Hopkins identifies with. While he is troubled by the destructive power of nature, his attitude to it, at least as it is expressed by the persona of the companion poem to 'Heaven-Haven', is to face it directly and uncompromisingly, without an obscuring veil and without seeking any form of monastic refuge: 'I must hunt down the prize | Where my heart lists.' The persona's 'heart lists'; it desires and goes into battle in this hostile place to fulfil its desire.

The dangers of Arctic exploration were brought home to the British public in 1858 with the sensational discovery of the remains of Sir John Franklin's ill-fated expedition, which had set out in 1845 to find the north-west passage. This grisly discovery inspired Sir Edwin Landseer's painting *Man Proposes, God Disposes* (1863–4), which Hopkins would have seen in the Royal Academy exhibition for 1864 a few days before he wrote the poem (*J.* 31). The Arctic setting of Hopkins's poem represents nature at its most treacherous, while his perception of it, by which he intends to distinguish 'the eagle's bulk' and the 'roll' of the setting seas, would constitute a kind of dominion over it. Indeed such simple acts of perception were for Victorian imperialist adventurers literally a form of mastery. The accepted convention amongst Europeans was that territory could be claimed for one's country by simply seeing, recording, and naming it before any other Westerner had done so. In 1860, for example, Captain John Speke named the great reservoir of the Nile he had discovered a few years earlier Lake Victoria and in 1864 Samuel Baker discovered and named Albert Lake, another body of water that had been known to indigenous Africans for millennia. Hopkins would have been familiar with this imperialist convention from his reading of Speke's *Journal of the Discovery of the Source of the Nile* (1863) in the months before he wrote 'I must hunt down the prize' (*J.* 21). The explorer persona of the poem not only provides a mouthpiece for Hopkins's resolve to discover the truth of natural phenomena, however difficult this may be; it also dramatizes a proprietary attitude to nature, a desire in some sense to own it.

In a playful letter to his friend Baillie in July 1863, Hopkins outlines a pattern of passionate appropriation, of enthusiastically making things his own, that he brings to his observations of nature:

> There are the most deliciously graceful Giottesque ashes (should one say *ashs*?) here – I do not mean Giottesque though, Peruginesque, Fra-Angelical(!), in Raphael's earlier manner. I think I have told you that I have particular periods of admiration for particular things in Nature; for a certain time I am astonished at the beauty of a tree, shape, effect etc, then when the passion, so to speak, has subsided, it is consigned to my treasury of explored beauty, and acknowledged with admiration and interest ever after, while something new takes its place in my enthusiasm. (*L3* 202)

Hopkins sees his understanding and appreciation of particular natural phenomena to culminate in the ownership of 'my treasury of explored beauty'. He regards them as a collection of valuables to be privately cherished and savoured. The ash trees are assimilated into Hopkins's 'treasury' by being aestheticized in the manner of John Ruskin, understood in relation to Italian paintings of the thirteenth to sixteenth centuries. While the nature observations of the journals are rather more sober and methodical, they nevertheless demonstrate this determination to describe nature independently, to draw it into his own terms.

Why does Hopkins feel the need to reach his own understandings of natural phenomena and in this way take possession of them? More than simply indicating his intellectual independence, it suggests that he was not happy with the way that nature was understood by his contemporaries. Both 'I must hunt down the prize' and its companion 'Heaven-Haven' share the same broad vision of an inhospitable storm-ridden nature, which they oppose with complementary attitudes, as one tries to conquer it, the other to avoid it entirely. Nature is by degrees represented as the same in the England of 'Heaven-Haven' as in the Arctic of its companion poem, hostile not only to human comfort and survival but to the effort to find meaning in it. This vision of a cruelly indifferent nature is a problem for Hopkins, indeed one that will provoke him into writing his longest and most radical poem, after the shipwreck of the *Deutschland* in a storm at sea in 1875 made its crew and passengers 'the prey of the gales' (*P.* 28, st. 24).

It is not only because they recalled the recent grisly discovery of the Franklin camp that bleak Arctic representations of nature were topical for the Victorian public of the early 1860s. Landseer's *Man Proposes, God Disposes,* which depicts two polar bears mauling the remains of an Arctic expedition, also presents a powerful emblem of Darwinian nature. Darwin's *The Origin of Species* appeared in 1859, a year after the remains of the Franklin expedition were discovered, and Landseer's painting draws the two together in a vision of a natural world that is cruelly indifferent to human endeavours and hopes. While speculative theories and observations about biological evolution, the idea that the types of animals and plants in nature are not fixed but change over time, gathered a popular audience in the 1840s and 1850s, it is only with the publication of *The Origin of Species* that a scientifically acceptable mechanism was offered to explain how such radical change could occur. This was the principle of natural selection, which saw that creatures were in competition with one another for the limited means of sustaining life and continuing their species. This competitive environment favours differences between individuals within species and species themselves that give them an advantage over others that helps them survive and breed. Nature, far from being fixed once and for all by God at the Creation, is defined by constant change, as new subspecies and then new species come into being over time, while others become extinct.

What Hopkins finds most disagreeable in post-Darwinian visions of nature is not the predatory 'Nature, red in tooth and claw' it gave credence to and that so disturbed Tennyson,[3] but more fundamentally that they make accident and flux rather than order and form the governing principles of nature. He makes this clear in his 1867 Oxford essay on 'The Probable Future of Metaphysics': 'one sees that the ideas so rife now of a continuity without fixed points, not to say *saltus* or breaks, of development in one chain of necessity, of species having no absolute types and only accidentally fixed, all this is a philosophy of flux' (*J.* 120). This vision of fluctuous nature is emblematized in the poem 'Heaven-Haven' by the bleak and vicious randomness of 'sharp and sided hail' (*P.* 9). The Darwinian 'philosophy of flux' directly opposes the sort of ordered theocentric cosmology that Hopkins outlines in 'Let me be to Thee'. It attacks the principles of harmony and design in the universe that this poem is so anxious to assert. In particular, Darwinism is a radical threat to the biblical understanding of nature, the idea that species were 'fixed' as 'absolute types' at the Creation. It is, in other words, a direct affront to the doctrine of Natural Theology, which maintains that we can comprehend the existence and nature of God by observing the details of the world he created. Its most important and widely read statement in the nineteenth century was William Paley's *Natural Theology; or, Evidences of the Existence and Attributes of the Deity, Collected from the Appearances of Nature* (1802). The representations of nature in Hopkins's companion poems and Landseer's painting are far removed from Paley's joyous and harmonious vision: 'The air, the earth, the water, teem with delighted existence. In a spring noon, or a summer evening, on whichever side I turn my eyes, myriads of happy beings crowd upon my view. "The insect youth are on the wing."'[4] For Paley the earth is crowded with happy and immaculately designed creatures, each of which testify to the power and goodness of their Creator. Everything in nature has inherent significance here, a meaning that enhances our understanding of the Creator's morally perfect and omnipotent nature.

Hopkins's careful scrutiny of particular natural phenomena effectively *reterritorializes* nature. His efforts in the journals and poetry to establish their defining form take them out of current, principally Darwinian, contexts of understanding and deliver them into the sanctuary of his own natural theological territory. Thus, for instance, in the 1877 poem 'Spring' the heightened flux of this season is quarantined from the Darwinian 'philosophy of flux' by being referred back to a Paleyan delighted and delightful Creation:

> What is all this juice and all this joy?
>   A strain of the earth's sweet being in the beginning
> In Eden garden . . .
>
> (*P*. 33)

Similarly, another poem on spring, from 1878, describes nature during the month of May, Mary's month, as 'The May Magnificat', a hymn to the Virgin. The final stanza of the poem sums up spring as 'This ecstasy all through mothering earth' (*P*. 42). The word 'ecstasy' is a curious choice here, as it usually refers to the state in which a person passes out of finite selfhood, transcends her or his natural state. The dynamism and joy of nature during May is, in other words, described as a *supernatural* rapture. The use of the word 'ecstasy' to describe nature marks the distance that Hopkins takes from the purely naturalistic explanations that Darwin and his peers were offering at the time. The 1877 poem 'Pied Beauty' focuses upon the very flux and variety of nature that in Darwinian terms indicates the instability of a constantly evolving nature, in order to assert that, on the contrary, it all evidences the underlying stable principle of the Creator:

> All things counter, original, spare, strange;
>   Whatever is fickle, freckled (who knows how?)
>   With swift, slow; sweet, sour; adazzle, dim;
> He fathers-forth whose beauty is past change:
>   Praise him.
>
> (P. 37)

In such poems as this Hopkins resacralizes nature. He wants to win over nature to his vision of order, to the Christ-centred cosmology he develops throughout his writings. The early poem 'Let me be to Thee as the circling bird' describes this pattern of gathering the phenomena of nature into a unifying vision, a harmonious relation with their Creator. The poem's curious pattern of concentricity is imperial, designating a fixed and eternal centre that moves outward to draw in the territories of nature and humanity, a colonizing impulse that is as we have seen dramatized in 'I must hunt down the prize'.

Viewed from the perspective of the colonizer, imperialism extends the principle of home to alien territory. The imperial sweep of the Pythagorean cosmology in 'Let me be to Thee', which contrasts so markedly with the alienating and fractured experiences of the world recorded in other poems from 1865, allows Hopkins to feel at home in the world. Home is for him not the 'Heaven-Haven' outlined in the early poem of that name, an artificial refuge achieved by turning one's back on the world, but rather what he refers to in the final stanza of 'The Wreck of the *Deutschland*' as 'the heaven-haven of the reward' (*P.* 28, st. 35), which is achieved as a consequence of 'Hurling the haven behind' (st. 13). The 'reward' in this poem, like 'the prize' in 'I must hunt down the prize', is earned by engaging actively with all that the world confronts him with, however unsympathetic or hostile it may seem to be to his beliefs. 'Let me be to Thee as the circling bird' states the poët's desire to find a place within a theocentric cosmology and outlines the integrated 'science' that he will develop through his new Catholic belief. His project can be glossed with Novalis's observation that 'Philosophy is really homesickness, an urge to be at home everywhere'.[5] While he formulates this 'science' most definitively three years later in his metaphysic of 'inscape', Hopkins's radical impulse to find order and certainty in the world and his experience of it can be traced back to his earliest writings on language and nature in the diaries and journals, which are the subject of the next chapter.

3

Words and Things

While Hopkins's early diaries (1862–6) and journals (1866–75) are best known for their observations of nature, most of the earliest surviving diary entries are concerned with words, the main medium in which the later observations are made. It is as if Hopkins feels the need to establish the reliability of his medium before he can employ it confidently in his later notes on natural phenomena. The first of Hopkins's surviving diary entries records complications in his schoolboy friendships. The second, which dates from 24 September 1863, when he was at Oxford, is about language. It is incomplete, but shows his efforts to trace relations between words that refer to the idea of growth in nature: 'growth, anything growing vigorously, blooming it may be, but yet producing fruit. Hence *mead* in the sense of meadow, or *meadow*, mean a field of fresh vegetation. *Mead* the drink and *meat*, (active forms from the same root,) are so called from strengthening, nourishing' (*J.* 4). There are, of course, all manner of words that have meanings associated with the idea of growth, but Hopkins restricts his discussion to those that share the sequence of letters *mea*. These letters are correlated with the idea of growth that is also common to these words, while their other letters mark their differences in meanings, specifying them as various aspects or extensions of their shared general idea.

Hopkins's interest in such relationships between the formal nature of words, their actual sequences of letters and sounds, and the objective world of nature they claim to represent is part of his larger concern with perception and epistemology, the branch of philosophy that asks how and what we can know. The last chapter noted that the young Hopkins was wary of the centralizing subjective perspective that the mind brings to its perceptions of the outside world: 'The earth and heaven, so little known,|Are measured outwards from my breast' (*P.* 130). This makes it very difficult to know how far we can trust that our perceptions are accurate representations of real objects and not just the constructions of our minds:

> It was a hard thing to undo this knot.
> The rainbow shines, but only in the thought
> Of him that looks. Yet not in that alone,
> For who makes rainbows by invention?
>
> (*P.* 91)

In this extract from an unfinished poem written in August 1864, the insubstantial phenomenon of the rainbow, which consists of light reflected and refracted by water vapour, suggests that all that we see may be just a play of light, mere appearances without substance. Nevertheless it does allow that we can have some grasp on reality; 'for who makes rainbows by invention?' This rhetorical question implies that, whatever we make of our subjective perception of the rainbow, it must be based in some external sensory stimulus, in this case, the light that hits the eye.

Many of Hopkins's earliest explorations of language focus upon the direct relation that some words have to this datum of sense experience by which the concrete world makes itself known to us. In the following diary entry from 1863 Hopkins lists a series of onomatopoeic words that replicate the very sounds that are made by rubbing up against the concrete world:

> *Grind, gride, gird, grit, groat, grate, greet, κρούειν, crush, crash, κροτεῖν* etc.
>
> Original meaning to *strike, rub,* particularly *together*. That which is produced by such means is the *grit,* the *groats* or crumbs, like *fragmentum* from *frangere, bit* from *bite. Crumb, crumble* perhaps akin. To *greet,* to strike the hands together(?). *Greet,* grief, wearing, *tribulation. Grief* possibly connected. *Gruff,* with a sound as of two things rubbing together. I believe these words to be onomatopoetic. *Gr* common to them all representing a particular sound. In fact I think the onomatopoetic theory has not had a fair chance. Cf. *Crack, creak, croak, crake, graculus, crackle.* These must be onomatopoetic. (*J.* 5)

The 'sound as of two things rubbing together' that these onomatopoeic words mean and make serves to highlight Hopkins's hopes for language as a medium that allows direct contact and communication between the subject (or self) and the concrete object world. The word 'onomatopoetic', as Hopkins would have known from his classics studies, comes from the Greek for 'name-making' and indicates that the Greeks thought that words were formed in this imitative manner. Hence 'the onomatopoetic theory' that he believes 'has not had a fair chance' maintains that all words originate as onomatopoeia, springing from and replicating direct experience of the concrete world: *'Foot, pes* (*ped-is*) *ποῦσ* (*ποδ-ός*), *pada, pad, pat* etc. Origin onomatapoetic, describing sound of foot-fall' (*J*. 7).

The subjective currency of language, the fact that we can think and speak it, is of course self-evident. What Hopkins is most concerned to establish in his early diaries is the traffic that language has with the outside world, and hence its status as a medium that allows us access to this world. This is, as we have seen, why many of his word lists in the early diaries focus upon onomatopoeic words, examples of language that engage most self-evidently and ostentatiously with concrete phenomena: *'slip, slipper, slop, slabby* (muddy), *slide,* perhaps *slope . . .'* (*J*. 9), *'fillip, flip, cf. flap, flob'* (*J*. 12), *'Spuere, spit, spuma, spume, spoom, spawn, spittle, spatter, spot, sputter'* (*J*. 16). But Hopkins wants language to give him access to an objective reality that extends beyond simple sounds of grinding, slopping, and spitting. Such sounds give information about separate sense experiences, isolated facts, but, as their arrangement in the word lists show, Hopkins is interested in the way that they acquire meaning through their *relations* with other words: *'Fluster* variation of *flutter. Flatter* probably to fan with applause, to flutter up – or else to inflate, blow out' (*J*. 11).

Hopkins was as a young man preoccupied with the idea of relation and with establishing relations between things. This is evident not only in the word lists and other notes on language in the early diaries, but in his observations of nature and his speculations on philosophy and aesthetics in the essays he wrote as an undergraduate at Oxford. Truth for Hopkins is found not in isolated facts but in the way that they relate to each other to form ideas. In his early Oxford essays he argues against contemporary philosophies and scientific methodologies that see nature, not in terms of its relations, but simply as more or less disconnected matter. His great enemies are the complementary philosophies of atomism and positivism. Atomism sees nature to consist ultimately of irreducible atoms or particles of matter in motion. It is a form of materialism, as it asserts that all reality is made up of matter. Positivism maintains that the only knowledge we can have comes from our sense impressions of such matter – that is, of particular things we can see, hear, smell, taste, and touch. Such sense perceptions of particulars can, according to positivism, be added together to make generalizations about specific phenomena. This is the method that was employed and promoted by Darwinian biology, which in its turn offered a purely materialistic explanation of organic nature.

In his 1867 essay on 'The Probably Future of Metaphysics', Hopkins describes the positivist idea of knowledge that was current at the time as 'the prevalent principle that knowledge is from the birth upwards, is a history of growth, and mounts from the part to the whole' (*J.* 120). But simply adding such particulars together does not, according to Hopkins, yield an understanding of the whole. He argues that knowledge does not build in this way 'from the part to the whole', but rather that the part, the particular, gains its significance only through its relation to the whole, the idea of the specific phenomenon it instances. Metaphysics is for Hopkins the branch of knowledge that creates and explores ideas, hence: 'It will always be possible to shew how science is atomic, not to be grasped and held together, "scopeless", without metaphysics: this alone gives meaning to laws and sequences and causes and developments – things which stand in a position so peculiar that we can neither say of them they hold in nature whether the mind sees them or not nor again that they are found by the mind because it first put them there' (*J.* 118). The problem of perception that he states in the early poetic fragment on the rainbow is overcome through his principle of the idea. Whether or not it is seen to exist only in the mind, or in nature as well, an overarching idea is needed to bring particulars into relation with each other and so give them meaning as parts of a whole: 'the Idea is only given – whatever may be the actual form education takes – from the whole downwards to the parts' (*J.* 120). Despite the fact that we first come across objects through our senses in the form of particulars (this is, I think, what Hopkins means here by 'the actual form education takes'), the idea of the thing is, he believes, what enables us to understand such particulars. Thus, for example, when we see a mass of flat thin green things with curved outlines amongst some brownish sticks on top of a larger brownish cylindrical form, we think of it immediately as a tree rather than as lots of separate and unrelated objects, such as leaves, trunk, and bark, or, more fundamentally still, as bare attributes or qualities, such as brownness, greenness, roundness, straightness, thickness, thinness, and so on. But then even these most basic observations would not be possible, as they are themselves ideas that gain their significance only in relation to other ideas. Ideas are for Hopkins the way in which particulars are drawn together in a relation, as a whole that is greater than its parts. As the early diary entry on 'mead' and 'meadow' shows, Hopkins looks to both language and nature to establish relations between their respective phenomena and so demonstrate the aptness of language for representing nature.

The early word lists indicate Hopkins's desire to establish not only that language participates directly in the concrete sounds that objects produce but also that it recognizes actual relationships between such phenomena. In the passage cited earlier, for instance, the word 'Grind' embodies a key or core meaning ('to *strike, rub,* particularly *together*') and sound ('*Gr*'), which, as Hopkins presents it, generates a series of variants that allow distinctions and relations to be observed between phenomena: 'That which is produced by such means is the *grit,* the *groats* or crumbs, like *fragmentum* from *frangere, bit* from *bite*' (*J.* 5). Many of the early notes on language explore the relations between words by speculatively linking their sounds with their possible Greek, Latin, or Anglo-Saxon etymologies: '*Shaw* in old English means shade of trees, cover, underwood etc. With it are connected *shadow, shade, shed, shelter, shield*' (*J.* 12). The relationship between such words is not directly onomatopoeic (although in this example the muffled sound 'sh' suggests an analogy to the softened light of shadow and shade), but their shared letters and sounds do give them a family resemblance to one another. Such sequences, like the onomatopoeic word lists, look to establish an underlying logic or pattern that links words and so reveals a series of connections that draw together and organize the phenomena they refer to around a central idea.

Hopkins wishes to establish that words function, not as atoms of matter, in the manner of the isolated onomatopoeic word sound, but as parts of integrated wholes of meaning. He wants to see them, not as noises, but as music. So, for example, he treats the series *'Flick, fillip, flip, fleck, flake'* as a gradation of shared principles of sound and meaning that can be described accordingly by analogy with a musical scale: 'To *fleck* is the next tone above flick, still meaning to touch or strike lightly . . . but in a broader less slight manner' (*J.* 11). The reference to 'tone' here indicates that Hopkins thinks of such word lists as sets of harmonious relations. This is an idea of language that evidently remained with him. In his notes for a lecture on 'Rhythm and the other Structural Parts of Rhetoric – Verse', which he delivered during his brief tenure as Professor of Rhetoric at Manresa House, Roehampton, between September 1873 and July 1874, Hopkins employs the musical analogy of the scale in referring to 'neighbouring vowels in one of the vowel scales, as *love* and *of* . . . or *love* and *prove* . . . or *bear* and *near*' (*J.* 285). Furthermore, he sees such relations between groups of words to harmonize and rhyme with other such groups: 'wade : waddle = stride : straddle = swathe : swaddle = ming (mix) : mingle etc.' (*J.* 25).

The musical analogies that Hopkins uses to describe the patterns he finds amongst words are used also in his journals to describe colours in nature: 'I counted in a bright rainbow two, perhaps three | complete octaves, that is | three, perhaps four | strikings of the keynote or nethermost red, counting from the outermost red rim' (*J.* 237). He refers similarly to 'the chord of colour' of a lily (*J.* 260), a metaphor that is developed in another journal entry to describe the effect of the purple tones of a lake in Switzerland: 'the purple expressing the rose of the chord to the eye (– in the same way as the same colour in a rose fading expresses the blue of the chord – the converse case: in fact it may perhaps be generalised that when this happens the modulation in question is the flat of the next term and not the sharp of the former one)' (*J.* 170).[1]

The respective analogies that Hopkins makes of the musical scale to the spectrum of colour in nature and the graduated sounds and meanings of the word lists in the early diaries imply a principle of Pythagorean order and pattern in nature and language. His references to the sounds and meanings of words in musical terms of tones and scales, and indeed his arrangement of them in such graduated sequences in the word lists, indicate that he thinks of them abstractly as a series of *values* that have a harmonious relation to one another. Pythagoreanism sees the universe as grounded in such abstract relations of numerical values as the proportionate distances between the concentric orbits of planets or between the lengths of taut strings and the notes they can produce. By establishing that words relate to each other in an abstract manner as different values of sound and meaning, Hopkins sees language as structurally parallel to phenomena that are grounded in analogous relations of value, such as those of the spectra of colour in nature. The grounds of Hopkins's faith in this analogy between nature and language is made explicit in 'Let me be to Thee as the circling bird' (*P.* 19).

'Let me be to Thee' expresses the poet's Pythagorean hopes, not only for nature, as was discussed in the last chapter, but for language also. The poem begins with the persona's wish to be like the bird and bat, which each express themselves in 'a changeless note'. The cry of the bat, like that of some birds, is an eerie and lonely sound. The sounds made by each of the creatures in the poem are, like the sounds of individual words, isolated and largely unmeaning until they are brought into relation with other such sounds. But, unlike the word lists, in which the sound and significance of each word are relative to each of the other words in the list, the creatures' sounds are harmonized by being brought into relation with an absolute principle, the 'authentic cadence' that God represents. For the persona of the poem, whose distinctive mode of expression parallel to that of the bird and the bat is language, this music is found 'in a common word'. The poem's little story about the bird's and the bat's cries presents a hopeful allegory of human language. The 'common word' that brings all into Pythagorean order is, of course, revealed in the last line of the poem as 'Love' or God. The implication here is that human language, like the sounds made by the creatures here, acquires its meaning through its ultimate relation to its 'dominant', to the transcendental signified of God or the Word, the anchor and guarantor of all meaning. This, in turn, ensures that language functions as a reliable medium, which allows us to grasp the truth of the outside world. The 'common word' is Christ, a medium between the human and the divine that participates in both. Just as, according to Christian doctrine, God became man in the figure of Jesus Christ so that all mankind could be saved, the Word or *Logos* becomes here 'a common word' and so secures human language.

Just as Hopkins sees onomatopoeia as demonstrating that language can directly represent and participate in the concrete reality of sense experience – that is, the sounds of things – he similarly sees the relations between words he assembles in his word lists as representing actual relations between things in the world. While this idea emerges cautiously in the early diaries as a hopeful hypothesis that he appears to be testing and trying to establish, he employs it confidently in the nature observations in the journals and it becomes foundational for his later poetry. A couple of lines from the late poem 'That Nature is a Heraclitean Fire and of the comfort of the Resurrection' serve as an example of this distinctive conception of language: 'in pool and rutpeel parches | Squandering ooze to squeezed dough, crust, dust; stanches, starches' (*P.* 72). This sequence describes a pool of water drying into mud and then dust, a process that is made more rapid by the action of the wind. But the meaning here, as elsewhere in Hopkins's poetry, is not obvious and easy to discover on a first reading. The reason for this is not any inadequacy on the reader's part, but simply Hopkins's attitude to language and how it works (or perhaps, more accurately, how he works it). There are to be found in Hopkins's poetry, as he observes to Bridges, 'excellences higher than clearness at a first reading' (*L1* 54). The sequence from the 'Heraclitean Fire' sonnet demonstrates the way that he often treats words abstractly as relative sound values, so that our first sense of what they mean comes, not from their literal sense, their dictionary definitions, but, as was observed of 'To seem the stranger' (*P.* 66) in Chapter 1, through the relations of their spoken sounds. The full long vowel sound of the word 'pool' in the first line thins to 'peel' just as that of 'ooze' thins to 'squeezed' as the liquid mud coagulates in the more substantive tongue-thickening word 'dough', before the proliferation of hard consonants and short vowel sounds in the crisp dessication of 'crust' and then 'dust'. The final clause, which occurs after the semicolon and establishes the rhyme with the previous line, sums up the preceding sequence: 'stanches, starches'. Even as he describes disintegration, as the liquid unity of a puddle degrades into the atomism of dust, Hopkins brings to the fore the unity of process, of an overarching idea that describes the principle of change here.

Viewed from the perspective offered by the lines from the 'Heraclitean Fire' sonnet, the early word lists look like an apprenticeship in poetry, an exercise in honing the sharpness and precision of words ready for later use. Thus, for example, in the sequence '*Grind, gride, gird, grit, groat, grate, greet*', each word sound does indeed rub up against the others alongside it, refining the precise sense that belongs to it and distinguishing it from all the other similar sounding and meaning words. Hopkins continues this preparation for poetry in the nature observations. He draws upon his armoury of crisply differentiated and neatly arranged sets of words to describe and define particular natural phenomena, as in the following journal entry for 11 July 1866: 'Oats: hoary blue-green sheaths and stalks, prettily shadow-stroked spikes of pale green grain' (*J.* 144). This statement is like a scientific formula. The placement of the colon gives it the structure of an equation, with a name on one side and the pared-down set of terms that define it on the other. The precision and crispness of the words here, which are reminiscent of the word lists, are consistent not only with scientific description but also with poetry, especially when it is read aloud. The word 'Oats' is little more than a stressed long vowel sound, and in the description that follows it the word seems to generate a graduated series of similar, stressed, vowel sounds. It draws upon what Hopkins refers to later as 'the vowel scales' in a way that echoes the word lists and anticipates his later poetry. Just as Hopkins's early speculative writings on language aim to discover patterns of sound and meaning that bring particular words into relation with one another and their referents, so also in his notes on nature he wishes to establish the patterns, the relations between the parts, that define such things as plants, landscapes, clouds, sunsets, and bodies of water. He relies upon his private armoury of words to outline and fix the patterns of particularity in nature, often, as with the entry on 'Oats', with a haiku-like economy, precision, and sober charm.

Immediately after the sentence on 'Oats' in this journal entry, as if he is seeking to establish the relation between two similar sounding words in the manner of the word lists, Hopkins moves on to 'Oaks: the organisation of this tree is difficult. Speaking generally no doubt the determining planes are concentric, a system of brief contiguous and continuous tangents, whereas those of the cedar would roughly be called horizontals and those of the beech radiating but modified by droop and by a screw-set towards jutting points' (*J.* 144). Parallel to the way he presents words in the word lists as analogous to musical scales, Hopkins specifies the relations between particular natural phenomena here in terms of the other great Pythagorean principle of form, that of geometry: the pure and eternal abstraction of planes, tangents, and concentric circles. A few days later, on 19 July, he announces:

> I have now found the law of the oak leaves. It is of platter-shaped stars altogether; the leaves lie close like pages, packed, and as if drawn tightly to. But these old packs, which lie at the end of their twigs, throw out now long shoots alternately and slimly leaved, looking like bright keys. All the sprays but markedly these ones shape out and as it were embrace greater circles and the dip and toss of these make the wider and less organic articulations of the tree. (*J.* 146)

The leaves are further assimilated here to the geometrical relations of 'greater circles' but not in the static manner associated with Pythagorean geometry, for they actively 'shape out' such form. The parallel placement of these sprays of leaves on different horizontal planes is described dynamically as a 'dip and toss'. They also 'throw out now long shoots alternately and slimly leaved'. The dynamic effect belongs to the way the packs of leaves figuratively throw their shoots of leaves at the eye, as if this dumb natural phenomenon is appealing to the viewer to recognize and understand it.

Hopkins is able finally to specify 'the law of the oak leaves', not as a static formula, akin to a scientific description or diagram of a typical spray of leaves, but as a series of dynamic relations. This indicates the influence of Aristotle, who, as mentioned in Chapter 1, understands organic form as a distinctive potential that is realized through the growth of the organism. In his development of Aristotle's principle, Hopkins sees form to be *expressed* by natural phenomena: 'A budded lime against the field wall: turn, pose, and counterpoint in the twigs and buds – the *form* speaking' (*J.* 163). On a visit to France in July 1867 he notes conversely that 'The trees were irregular, scarcely expressing form, and the aspens blotty, with several concentric outlines' (*J.* 147). Each creature in nature, according to the later poem 'As kingfishers catch fire', actively expresses itself, 'Selves – goes itself; *myself* it speaks and spells' (*P.* 57). This means that Hopkins need not fear that his perceptions of the outside world are, as he suggests in 'It was a hard thing to undo this knot' (*P.* 91), solipsistic – that is, the mere projection of his own ideas upon the world – for nature is seen actively to reach out expressively to meet our active powers of perception. Indeed nature, it seems, needs human perception, for, as Hopkins writes in the poem 'Ribblesdale', the Earth has 'no tongue' and 'canst but only be': 'And what is Earth's eye, tongue, or heart else, where | Else, but in dear and dogged man?' (*P.* 58).

The leaves of the oak tree become legible for Hopkins in terms of those of the book: 'the leaves lie close like pages, packed, and as if drawn tightly to' (*J.* 146). In his reading of this phenomenon it is the parallel and intersecting circles described by each such bunch of leaves that, Hopkins concludes, 'make the wider and less organic articulations of the tree', finally articulating or joining together the parts that originally made 'the organisation of this tree ... difficult' for him. This pattern of circles articulates the parts of the tree as if they were carefully chosen words in a sentence. The play on the idea of articulation is brought to the fore in the poems mentioned earlier: 'Ribblesdale', which asserts directly that the Earth needs man to be its 'tongue', and 'As kingfishers catch fire', where nature 'spells' itself (rather than utters its identity and source outright in the manner of the tall nun in 'The Wreck of the *Deutschland*'). The implication of this metaphor of spelling is that each natural phenomenon gives to human perception the letters that comprise it and so depends upon the mind to put such parts together, to articulate it, so that they join up to spell a name, the word that represents the unifying idea of the creature's distinctive nature. Hopkins's exploratory approach to nature in the diaries and journals is parallelled and indeed facilitated by his approach to language in the early word lists. In each case he studies a particular phenomenon, whether it be words starting with the letters '*Gr*' or the leaves of the oak tree, until he understands its form, the group of relations that defines it. Starting from a position of doubt and even scepticism about human perception, Hopkins recognizes in language the medium between us and the world, and sees in its structures the grounds for knowledge of the world.

4

Being

The early diaries and the journals record Hopkins wrestling with protean nature to 'law out' its forms. At the same time as he is exploring the particular phenomena of nature and language in this way he is also at work building his own metaphysic: his own integrated theory of what constitutes distinct objects in the world, what their relations to one another are, and how we can know them. In so doing he battles against the hostile forces of contemporary thought that he outlines in 'The Probable Future of Metaphysics' and that were introduced earlier – namely, the materialist theories of atomism and positivism, and the recent application and extension of these ideas in Darwinian evolution, 'the ideas so rife now of a continuity without fixed points . . . of species having no absolute types and only accidentally fixed'. As well as summing up this current evolutionary philosophy, his essay also anticipates the type of thought that may oppose it in the future: 'all this is a philosophy of flux opposed to Platonism and can call out nothing but Platonism against it. And this, or to speak more correctly Realism, is perhaps soon to return' (*J.* 120). But Hopkins is not content simply to leave it to others to contest the contemporary 'philosophy of flux'. In his early Oxford and Birmingham essays and notes he draws upon the long tradition of idealist thought to develop his metaphysic of 'instress' and 'inscape', which he states first and most fully in some 1868 notes on the Presocratic philosopher Parmenides.

The Pythagoreanism announced in 'Let me be to Thee' is developed in several of the undergraduate essays. 'The Probable Future of Metaphysics' offers a succinct account of how Hopkins draws upon it to 'challenge the prevalent philosophy of continuity or flux':

> To the prevalent philosophy and science nature is a string all the differences in which are really chromatic but certain places in it have become accidentally fixed and the series of fixed points becomes an arbitrary scale. The new Realism will maintain that in musical strings the roots of chords, to use technical wording, are mathematically fixed and give a standard by which to fix all the notes of the appropriate scale: when points between these are sounded the ear is annoyed by a solecism, or to analyse deeper, the mind cannot grasp the notes of the scale and the intermediate sound in one conception; so also there are certain forms which have a great hold on the mind and are always reappearing and seem imperishable, such as the designs of Greek vases and lyres, the cone upon Indian shawls, the honeysuckle moulding, the fleur-de-lys, while every day we see designs both simple and elaborate which do not live and are at once forgotten; and some pictures we may long look at and never grasp or hold together, while the composition of others strikes the mind with a conception of unity which is never dislodged: and these things are inexplicable on the theory of pure chromatism or continuity – the forms have in some sense or other an absolute existence. It may be maintainable then that species are fixed and to be fixed only at definite distances in the string and that the developing principle will only act when the precise conditions are fulfilled. To ascertain these distances and to point out how they are to be mathematically or *quasi*-mathematically expressed will be one work of this metaphysic. (*J.* 120)

Hopkins bases his argument upon the fundamental Pythagorean discovery of the relation between the length of taut strings and the sounds they can make. He uses this as an analogy for forms in both nature, or God's Creation, and art, man's creations. Just as each note of the musical scale can be marked at a precise length of a taut string (as, for instance, in piano wires or the string instruments), so analogously each species in nature is for Hopkins a distinct form. He argues that, just as we can appreciate the mathematically determined forms of musical notes, and conversely find sounds between such notes irritating, so we are able to recognize certain definite forms in nature and in the fine arts to be fixed and essential and not the 'accidental' consequence of evolutionary process. Such forms are for Hopkins like musical notes, defined by proportion, a relation between their parts that furnishes the mind with the unity of the idea. Chapter 3 introduced the importance that Hopkins places upon relation and the way that parts are brought together in an idea. He explains that we dislike musical notes that are off key because they do not furnish the mind with such unity, 'the mind cannot grasp the notes of the scale and the intermediate sound in one conception'. Similarly, when it comes to visual material, he writes that there are 'some pictures [which] we may long look at and never grasp or hold together, while the composition of others strikes the mind with a conception of unity which is never dislodged.' Again, it is for Hopkins the relation of the parts that gives the unity of the idea, the form. The mind is for Hopkins an active principle able to recognize and enjoy such instances of form in nature and art. The idealized organic forms used in art, such as the 'Indian cone' (or paisley figure) and the *fleur-de-lys*, serve to highlight the mind's preadaption to appreciating the forms of nature, which are, as Hopkins explains in 'On the Origin of Beauty: A Platonic Dialogue', characterized by a proportionate mixture of regularity and irregularity. The 'Platonic Dialogue' gives the example of the fan of chestnut leaves, the beauty of which comes, not from 'the likeness of the leaves, but their likeness as thrown up by their difference in size', but then, not alone from such 'inequality, but the inequality as tempered by their regular diminishing . . . Nor their each having a diametrical opposite, but that opposite [leaf] being the least answering to themselves in the whole fan' (*J*. 93). The effect of this mixture of sameness and difference is a dynamic unity, a series of tensions between the parts that, as Hopkins's journal entry on the oak leaves serves to highlight, suggests movement: 'these old packs . . . throw out now long shoots alternately and slimly leaved.'

The recognition of form in nature and art is for Hopkins not just an aesthetic experience but an epistemological act, the recognition of a truth. He writes in his 1885 poem 'To what serves Mortal Beauty?' that mortal beauty, which could be seen to include not only the poem's main concern with human beauty but all the forms of biological nature, 'does this: keeps warm | Men's wits to the things that are; what good means' (*P*. 62). The experience of beauty is not for Hopkins frivolous, but the recognition of the real, that which *is*. It brings to the fore *being* itself. The perception of form in nature is for Hopkins the discovery of the truth of the Creation and so from his natural theological perspective a moral activity, an apprehension of the Creator, 'what good means'. The beautiful, the true, and the good all coincide here in Hopkins's idea of being. He formulates this radical principle most fully through his coinages of 'instress' and 'inscape' in his 1868 notes on Parmenides, the first Western philosopher to analyse the idea of Being, what it means to say that something *is*. The surviving fragments of Parmenides' philosophical poem, which are both incomplete and poetically suggestive, provide Hopkins with the stimulus and scope finally to crystallize his own distinctive metaphysic, his own version of the 'new Realism' he anticipates in 'The Probable Future of Metaphysics'.

Parmenides, who flourished around 480 BC, is the first idealist philosopher and the first philosopher to use a formal logical argument. He begins this argument with the simple, tautologous statement that 'Being is'.[1] From this he proceeds to deduce that Being must be consistent with itself and unchanging over time. It is for him an entirely stable and unified entity, which he accordingly describes as a sphere. This conception of Being entails conversely that all things that human beings refer to in terms of change and multiplicity must be illusory. He accordingly consigns all such things to 'mortal opinion' and labels them 'Not-being'. Hopkins, of course, does not dismiss these principles of flux and diversity but famously celebrates 'All things counter, original, spare, strange' (*P.* 37). Having studied Aristotle for several years at Oxford, he is not troubled by the apparently contradictory relation between Being and change that is so fundamental to Parmenides' thinking. Hopkins follows Aristotle in equating Being with form, which he understands not as the antithesis of change but rather as a potential that is realized *through* change, the thing that remains constant through movement and growth. Hopkins accentuates this dynamism in his conception of being as 'stress'.

We know from the word lists in the early diaries that Hopkins attends closely to the etymology and meanings of particular words. He clearly develops his term 'stress' from the fundamental mechanical sense of the word, which refers to a physical pressure or strain. His early unpublished notebook on mechanics demonstrates his understanding of mechanical stress,[2] while some of his journal entries indicate that he was not afraid to see nature as mechanical process: 'indeed all nature is mechanical, but then it is not seen that mechanics contain that which is beyond mechanics' (*J.* 252). A stress occurs in a material as a result of the resistance it offers to an outside force, as, for instance, when the weight of bricks pushes down upon a window lintel. The stress is the *resultant* of two forces – for example, that of the weight of the bricks pressing down and the residual strength and resilience of the strip of iron or stone that acts as the lintel. Furthermore, during the 1850s and 1860s mechanical stress was used by early energy physicists, principally James Clerk Maxwell, as an analogy for the effects of electricity and magnetism, so that, for example, the attraction and repulsion of magnets were explained in terms of a stress in the space between them, two forces that interact to form a single tension or stress. In a poem from 1876 Clerk Maxwell defines this concept in relation to Newtonian physics, which he sees it superseding:

> Both Action and Reaction now are gone.
> Just ere they vanished,
> Stress joined their hands in peace, and made them one.[3]

The mechanistic physics of Clerk Maxwell and his peers focused upon electricity and magnetism, and the ways in which they interact and indeed change from one into the other. This discovery of electromagnetism was just one of many around the middle of the nineteenth century that established that all the fundamental physical forces, including work, heat, light, and sound, could each be changed into one another. They were all accordingly theorized as different modes of 'energy', the abstract quantity that remains the same through such changes. The new physics theorized forms of energy as particular types of movement in a medium, so that, for example, sound could be understood as vibrations transmitted through the air, and light as wavelike patterns of energy that are propagated in a hypothetical medium, the luminiferous ether. An early essay from 1867, 'The Tests of a Progressive Science', (*JP* 181–2) and a late plan to write 'a sort of popular account of Light and the Ether' (*L2* 139) indicate that Hopkins was familiar with this understanding of light throughout his adult life. The analogy of mechanical stress, which was pioneered in electromagnetism, was used also to describe such other basic physical phenomena as sound, heat, and light. Hopkins, for instance, refers to 'the stress of the heat' in a journal entry for March 1871 on the phenomena of boiling and evaporation (*J.* 203–4). The spectacular developments in physics during the middle third of the century unified its phenomena around the energy principle and effectively universalized the mechanistic principle of stress, so furnishing Hopkins with the basis for his dynamic unifying principle of being or 'stress'.

In contrast to traditional ideas, which saw space as something empty through which bodies move, the new energy physics crowded the media of the air and the ether with the most remorselessly dynamic activity. This modern understanding of the physical world is reproduced in Hopkins's poem 'Duns Scotus's Oxford', where Oxford is introduced as an expanse of air that is full not so much of towers and branches as vibrations from sounds made by bells and birds: 'Towery city and branchy between towers; | Cuckoo-echoing, bell-swarmèd, lark-charmèd, rook-racked, river-rounded' (*P.* 44). This poem, like much of Hopkins's work, represents the world in the manner of the new mechanistic physics as a force plenum – that is, as completely full of energy manifest here in ceaseless movement. While contemporary biological science in the form of Darwinism was effectively undermining the grounds of natural theology, Hopkins looks to contemporary physical science to renew such grounds for belief. With his doctrine of 'stress', 'instress', and 'inscape', he makes 'mechanics contain that which is beyond mechanics'. At the time that Darwinism was felt to be sundering nature from the Creator and dissolving the harmony of the Creation in systemic conflict and instability, Hopkins was able to renew the unity of Creation through the dynamic principle of energy or stress and trace it back to God: 'The world is charged with the grandeur of God. | It will flame out, like shining from shook foil' (*P.* 31). God's grandeur is seen here to subsist in the world as a potential energy, which can become actual in a flash. Hopkins uses the word *stress* by analogy with its original meaning in mechanics to describe the internal state of objects, within each of which it inheres as an instance, an inner stress or 'instress'. His usage follows the complete broadening of the word's application in physics during the 1850s and 1860s so that it is for him a principle that not only informs things but exists between them and allows us knowledge of the world, a 'stem of stress between us and things to bear us out and carry the mind over' (*J*. 127).

That Hopkins felt the need to coin his terms 'instress' and 'inscape' rather than drawing upon existing philosophical language indicates that he meant them to bear new meanings, new ideas of being, form, and knowing. They are, however, not fully explained by him. He coins the terms 'instress' and 'inscape', just as he employs the words 'stress' and 'scapes', for his private use, so that, apart from the initial oblique exposition in the 'Parmenides' notes and some rare references in the poems and letters, he feels no need to explain or justify them. His huge unanticipated readership have accordingly been left to glean the meanings of these curious terms from their diverse applications in his writings on philosophy, theology, art, and nature.

Instress builds upon the principle of stress or being, and is accordingly dwelt upon in the 'Parmenides' notes, where in the process of inventing the concept Hopkins largely specifies its meaning. Whereas Parmenides sees Being as a sphere, a monolithic whole without any parts, Hopkins's principle of stress allows him to see it as similarly ubiquitous but as manifest in particular instances of being that are defined by their form. Hopkins glosses Parmenides' central concept as 'the unextended, foredrawn' (*J*. 128) -- that is, as the bounded and the coherent, that which is drawn into itself, within its limits. His own conception of being is clarified by his comments on Parmenides' description of Being as a sphere: 'He . . . may very well mean this as an analogy merely, especially as the comparison is to the outline and surface rather than to the inner flushness, the temper and equality of weight' (*J*. 128–9). There is for Hopkins more to form than just the outline that defines and contains the unity of a thing. Unity is not enforced by the prison of a boundary, the containing skin of a thing. Rather this 'foredrawn' quality is for Hopkins itself *informed* by 'the inner flushness', an energetic quality that he notes

Parmenides does not acknowledge in his analogy. Early in his notes on Parmenides Hopkins coins the term 'instress' and immediately glosses it as 'the flush and foredrawn' (*J*. 127). Being or form flushes a thing, in the manner of water rushing into a pool or the blood surging around the body.

In 'The Wreck of the *Deutschland*' Hopkins likens himself, his individual being, to a well:

> I steady as a water in a well, to a poise, to a pane,
> But roped with, always, all the way down from the tall
> Fells or flanks of the voel, a vein
> Of the gospel proffer, a pressure, a principle, Christ's gift.
>
> (*P*. 28, st. 4)

His writings are full of such hydrodynamic analogies for being. While in this extract the poet's finite being is represented by the well, the poem identifies the Being of God with the ocean. He is the

> master of the tides,
> Of the Yore-flood, of the year's fall;
> The recurb and the recovery of the gulf's sides,
> The girth of it and the wharf of it and the wall . . .
>
> (*P*. 28, st. 32)

The ocean suggests God's infinite Being, the source of all that *is*. As 'The Wreck of the *Deutschland*' serves to highlight, this ocean moves ceaselessly, constantly reiterating Hopkins's dynamic principle of Being. The main point of the analogy that the poem makes of the poet's being to the well is not the literal containment of this body of water, defined by the walls of the well, but the principle of 'flushness', the 'pressure' of the spring that sustains it and connects it to ultimate Being or God.

Synonymous with 'being' or energy, the quality of stress corresponds to the dynamic informing principle of 'flushness'. But, as the prefix added to the word to form his coinage 'instress' indicates, this flushness meets another principle, which works reciprocally to foredraw or draw it 'in'. The foredrawn is the principle that individualizes stress or being: 'The selfless self of self, most strange, most still, | Fast furled and all foredrawn to No or Yes' (*P*. 157). Inextricable from one another, the flushness of stress moves outwards, while the foredrawn quality draws it inwards, contains it, as a particular instance of being. Olive oil, the consistency of which balances its power of dispersion with that by which it draws together within its meniscus, provides a simple example of this phenomenon, which Hopkins uses to describe 'God's Grandeur' in the poem of that name: 'It gathers to a greatness, like the ooze of oil | Crushed' (*P*. 31). The greatness of the oil is its peculiar quality of coherence, its instress. Together, inseparable from one another, these two counterpoised principles form a particular type of tension or stress, a literally dynamic unity. This is Hopkins's basic principle of form, which he refers to in its more abstract mode as instress and its more concrete as inscape.

An instress is the pattern of 'stress or energy' (*S*. 137) that upholds an instance of being. As such, as something 'in' a particular being, it is not directly visible, but a principle of form that we can glean or, as Hopkins puts it in the journal entry on the waves discussed in Chapter 2, 'unpack,' from the appearances of a thing. He refers in this entry to such informatively patterned appearances as 'scapes': 'About all the turns of the scaping from the break and flooding of wave to its run out again I have not yet satisfied myself' (*J*. 223). Two years later, in August 1874, he describes the sequence in which such waves break and their remains wash back out to sea. He observes that the current that pulls the water back to the foredrawn unity of the sea is disclosed by its appearances, which, formed by the remaining froth from the broken waves, provide a good example of scapes; 'long dribble bubble-strings which trace its set and flow' (*J*. 251). The example of art, as in the following approving description of a painting by Briton Rivière, highlights the way in which the flow of the scapes can expressively mark the 'inscape': 'Leopards shewing the flow and slow spraying of the streams of spots down from the backbone and making this flow word-in and inscape the whole animal and even the group of them' (*J*. 244).

As the coinage itself indicates, inscape draws together Hopkins's respective principles of form and matter, of instress and the scapes in which it is manifest and visible. Indeed, it further clarifies his idea of form, the rationale behind instress, as a composite of the 'flushness' of both stress *and* resistant matter, for these are principles that each require the limits of form to define them and that find it through their dynamic interaction with one another, as each conditions or 'foredraws' the other. Thus, for example, the form of 'the Rhone glacier' is understood to be 'like bright-plucked water swaying in a pail'. In Hopkins's analogy the energy or stress meets the resistance of both the medium of water it courses through and the pail's sides, which together result in a counter-movement, a 'swaying'. The form of the huge and apparently immobile glacier is appreciated by Hopkins accordingly as 'swerved and inscaped strictly to the motion of the mass' (*J.* 178). Inscape is described here and elsewhere as 'swerved', the resultant of two directional forces, a dynamic poise that defines a thing, *holds* it in a distinctive unity: 'There is one notable dead tree in the N. W. corner of the nave, the inscape markedly holding its most simple and beautiful oneness up from the ground through a graceful swerve below (I think) the spring of branches up to the tops of the timber' (*J.* 215).

This passage on the 'notable dead tree' indicates that inscape describes a form that does not so much define or 'law out' a group or species as distinguish an individual phenomenon. In his early essay on 'The Probable Future of Metaphysics' Hopkins is keen to establish that 'the forms have in some sense or other an absolute existence' (*J.* 120). But, rather than simply adopting the philosophies of Plato and Aristotle that defend this principle (and that he knew well from his Oxford studies), Hopkins develops his doctrine of inscape, which is far more open to recognizing form in the full range of phenomena than the theories of his classical predecessors: 'All the world is full of inscape and chance left free to act falls into an order as well as purpose: looking out of my window I caught it in the random clods and broken heaps of snow made by the cast of a broom' (*J.* 230). Because his ontology follows Parmenides rather than Plato and Aristotle, privileging Being over specific form, Hopkins is concerned not so much with finding representative forms in nature as with being able fully to acknowledge *all* the forms of being, including the fleeting, unique, and accidental that have been largely disregarded by both classical and modern metaphysics. While in 'The Probable Future of Metaphysics' Hopkins opposes the Darwinian idea that species are 'accidentally fixed' with the Platonic idea that such defining forms are absolute and essential, he relaxes this opposition in his doctrine of 'inscape', where chance and accident, the contingent, are recognized as factors that can further define the form of particular phenomena: 'Sycomores grew on the slopes of the valley, scantily leaved, sharply quained and accidented by perhaps the valley winds, and often most gracefully inscaped' (*J.* 176). The classical idealism of Plato and realism of Aristotle would see these trees as less representative, less real, than sycomores that grow to type, unaffected by such accidental factors. Instead of judging them eccentric, Hopkins finds in them individual form, a distinctive inscape. Similarly, in the poem 'Binsey Poplars', Hopkins mourns a recently felled group of poplars, not because he sees them as examples of a generic form but rather as constituting a distinctive selfhood;

> Ten or twelve, only ten or twelve
>   Strokes of havoc únselve
>   The sweet especial scene.
>
> (*P.* 43)

So inscape is a principle of form that does not generalize phenomena but rather aims to recognize distinctiveness, not only of the species but of the individual and the group. This understanding of form explains why Hopkins was so receptive to the medieval philosopher John Duns Scotus when he first read him in 1872, four years after he formulated his doctrine of inscape: 'At this time I had first begun to get hold of the copy of Scotus on the Sentences in the Baddely library and was flush with a new stroke of enthusiasm . . . But just then when I took in any inscape of the sky or sea I thought of Scotus' (*J.* 221). The sky and the sea present the most fluctuous and various examples of Hopkins's dynamic principle of form: sunsets and sunrises, clouds and clear skies, lightning in the sky and storms at sea, starlit night skies and moonlit seascapes – myriad phenomena formed as particular interactions between basic physical qualities of air and water, light and darkness, heat and cold. Hopkins develops his own terms to describe such things as cloud and wave formations, and it is likely that his efforts to record their distinctive forms in numerous journal entries and drawings played a part in the development of his supple and inclusive principle of form. His concepts of instress and inscape allow him to recognize the ways in which such elements can come together, however fleetingly, and cohere in a distinctive unity. This idea of form as belonging not so much to a species as an individual thing or an event, such as a particular sunset or peculiar cloud drift, chimes in with Scotus' concept of *haeceittus*, which refers to a principle of singular essence or individuating difference, the 'thisness' of a thing.

Largely forgotten during the modern period of philosophy, which dates from Bacon and Descartes in the seventeenth century to Hegel in the nineteenth, Duns Scotus has emerged since Hopkins's time as an important thinker for critiques of classical and modern philosophy. A contemporary of Hopkins, the American founder of Semiotics C. S. Peirce, was greatly influenced by him in forming his realist theory of universals. Martin Heidegger wrote his doctoral thesis on Duns Scotus, who can be seen as foundational for this thinker's efforts to restore *Being* to the heart of philosophy. The concept of *haeceittus* has been renewed more recently by the French philosophers Gilles Deleuze and Félix Guattari to specify a principle of singular individuation, a becoming that is not teleological and that repudiates the transcendent and regulative categories that in classical and modern philosophy have served to organize and homogenize selfhood and experience. The way in which they interpret and develop *haeceittus* offers a suggestive gloss on Hopkins's concept of form. Deleuze and Guattari use *haeceittus* to define the individual body or phenomenon not by species or genus but by *affect*.[4] They identify the Scotist 'thisness' with the distinctive presence of a thing. As we saw earlier, in exploring the implications of the 'inscape[s] of the sky or sea' that Hopkins came to associate with Scotus, it is this sense of presence, of perceiving reality as an event rather than as a set of discrete fixed objects, that is central to his principle of inscape. This is the basis for Hopkins's mature theory of knowing, his epistemology, which is the subject of the next chapter.

5

Knowing

The quality of thisness and presence belonging to inscape registers affectively as an instress: 'We went up to the castle but not in: standing before the gateway I had an instress which only the true old work gives from the strong and noble inscape of the pointedarch' (*J*. 263). The term 'instress' still refers to the form of a thing as it was introduced earlier, the precise configuration of its being, but here, as something that the object 'gives' to the perceiver 'from the ... inscape', it is also epistemological; it furnishes us with knowledge of its being. We can accordingly distinguish the objective form of a thing as the *ontological* instress, which is given to and correspondingly 'felt' by the perceiver as an *affective* instress.

In the following passage on a 'running instress' Hopkins distinguishes affective instresses from purely subjective emotional states of mind and clarifies the ways in which they impress the perceiver with the singularity of their objects and events:

> On this walk I came to a cross road I had been at in the morning carrying it in another 'running instress'. I was surprised to recognise it and the moment I did it lost its present instress, breaking off from what had immediately gone before, and fell into the morning's ... And what is this running instress, so independent of at least the immediate scape of the thing, which unmistakeably distinguishes and individualises things? Not imposed outwards from the mind as for instance by melancholy or strong feeling: I easily distinguish that instress. I think it is this same running instress by which we identify or, better, test and refuse to identify with our various suggestions/ a thought which has just slipped from the mind at an interruption. (*J*. 215)

Hopkins differentiates an emotional instress, which originates with the subjective mind and can be imposed upon the outside world, from another kind of affect, an instress that allows us to recognize objective reality, 'which unmistakeably distinguishes and individualises things'. He likens the distinction we make to the peculiar case in which the mind, having momentarily forgotten a thought, nevertheless has an intuitive sense that the thoughts it suggests to itself as it tries to remember the original thought are not the right one. This instress is a thought that the mind receives through the presence of the object, an affect from without that registers in the mind immediately and involuntarily with a forceful conviction of reality and distinctive form.

Facilitated by the common principle of stress or being, an instress is given by the object and experienced by the subject. Perception effectively depends for Hopkins upon the active participation of both the subject and its object. The scapes of a thing gather or form in a manner that affects the perceiver with an instress of the inscape. Indeed, the forms of nature are seen to address themselves directly to us: 'The bluebells in your hand baffle you with their inscape, made to every sense' (*J*. 209). But, although inscapes are adapted to our means of perception, they do not reach us unless we are open and receptive to them: 'I thought how sadly beauty of inscape was unknown and buried away from simple people and yet how near at hand it was if they had eyes to see it and it could be called out everywhere again' (*J*. 221). Inscape is described here as a potential that, 'buried away', can be 'called out' from nature, realized or released through the active intervention of the beholder. In the poem 'Ribblesdale' this potential is implicit in the identification it makes of 'Earth' or nature with simple stress or being, for it 'canst but only be' (*P*. 58). Because it has 'no tongue to plead, no heart to feel', 'man' is required to be 'Earth's eye, tongue, or heart', to bring it to consciousness or instress it: to witness it with the eyes, to bear witness to it and lend it expression with the tongue, and 'to feel' it with the heart.

The 1877 poem 'Hurrahing in Harvest' dramatizes Hopkins's idea of perception as a collaboration between the subject and the object. Indeed, it does so in radical terms, which bring to the fore the divine source of stress that makes objects in nature active participants in perception. In these terms perception becomes a passionate communication between Christ, as he discloses his being through nature, and the poet:

> I walk, I lift up, I lift up heart, eyes,
> Down all that glory in the heavens to glean our Saviour;
> And, éyes, heárt, what looks, what lips yet gave you a
> Rapturous love's greeting of realer, of rounder replies?
>
> (*P*. 38)

The act of perception here mobilizes the whole body, which walks and lifts itself up towards the heavens. The catalogue of upward movements in the first line is balanced by the second, which brings 'all that glory in the heavens' perceived by the uplifted heart and eyes 'Down' to the level of human consciousness, so that it can 'glean our Saviour'. Much as in 'Ribblesdale', the eyes and the heart respectively represent the capacities for sensory perception and feeling that are necessary to receive an instress. Introduced in the first line, they reappear in the third literally bearing the marks of the stress they have received from recognizing Christ in the natural world. The instress of feeling they receive is described as a 'greeting', a courteous and passionate reply to their acknowledgement of Christ's being. The sestet of the poem examines further the consequences of this recognition:

> And the azurous hung hills are his world-wielding shoulder
> Majestic – as a stallion stalwart, very-violet-sweet! –
> These things, these things were here and but the beholder
> Wanting; which two when they once meet,
> The heart rears wings bold and bolder
> And hurls for him, O half hurls earth for him off under his feet.
>
> (*P*. 38)

The two parties to perception, the poet-beholder and the 'things', 'once meet'. Together they constitute a single instress. This meeting works to dissolve the distinction between the subject and the object, the beholder and the outside world, in a recognition of the source of their shared being in Christ. The beholder 'half hurls earth for him', a gesture that sympathetically if imperfectly echoes Christ's magisterial 'world-wielding'. While the heart 'rears wings', its consequent action is not an ethereal wingéd ascension to the heavens but the impetuous bodily movement of hurling that, as the last words of the poem suggest, results in a loss of the poet's footing. The poet does not transcend his finite nature, but remains close to the earth to which he earlier brought 'Down all that glory in the heavens'. The last lines of the poem present an image of instability. They suggest an undermining of the poet's secure identity as a unified subject, which is customarily defined against the object world of the earth, by the instress of Christ that is released through his encounter with nature. The secure first-person pronoun of the octave is superseded in the last line of the poem by the confusing use of third-person masculine pronouns, which blur the distinction between Christ and the poet in a manner that could be glossed with a line from the later sonnet 'That Nature is a Heraclitean Fire and of the comfort of the Resurrection': 'I am all at once what Christ is, since he was what I am' (*P*. 72).

An inscape is, as one of Hopkins's favourite metaphors for perception puts it, caught by the perceiver: 'I caught an inscape as flowing and well marked almost as the frosting on glass and slabs' (*J*. 227). A dynamic and forceful metaphor of reciprocity, it implies that nature throws inscapes at us. This trajectory of throwing and catching recalls the 'stem of stress between us and things to bear us out and carry the mind over' (*J*. 127) in the 'Parmenides' notes. 'The Windhover', the poem that Hopkins describes as 'the best thing I ever wrote' (*L1* 85) and that has yielded many contentious readings (indeed more commentary than any other of his works), records what has become his most celebrated catch:

I caught this morning morning's minion, king-
  dom of daylight's dauphin, dapple-dawn-drawn Falcon, in his riding
  Of the rolling level underneath him steady air, and striding
High there, how he rung upon the rein of a wimpling wing
In his ecstasy! then off, off forth on swing,
  As a skate's heel sweeps smooth on a bow-bend : the hurl and gliding
  Rebuffed the big wind. My heart in hiding
Stirred for a bird, – the achieve of, the mastery of the thing!

(*P*. 36)

What precisely is 'caught' here? It is not simply 'this morning', or 'morning's minion', phrases that are not separated by a comma (which would warrant the pause that we are apt to add when reading them aloud), but are run together, rather like the 'running instress' in the journal entry cited earlier, which 'fell into the morning's'. Indeed, the poem consistently runs its terms together. The first and second line of the octave are conjoined through their shared or 'run-on' word 'king- | dom', and subsequent lines end similarly in the middle of their clauses, as, for example, the third and fourth lines: 'and striding | High there'. Sequences of alliteration and assonance further draw together the flow of the words here: 'king | dom of daylight's dauphin, dapple-dawn-drawn Falcon'. What is caught in the six and a half lines of the opening sentence is an *event*, in relation to which all its terms are integral. This event is announced in the first line as a composite of a particular time ('this morning') and the creature whose being is run in with it ('morning's minion'). Indeed, the word 'minion' has all its letters contained within the word 'morning', thereby replicating the relation that the creature has to 'this morning' as its subordinate but defining principle (that which distinguishes it as *this* memorable morning). It is an echo, almost another repetition, of the word 'morning'. The highly stressed and repetitive sequence 'mórning mórning's mínion' marks an event that is emphatic and tautologous, an irreducible, epiphanic experience.

The opening sentence of the poem effectively runs its words and lines together into one long line that traces the bird's line of flight. This trajectory is determined by the creature's interactions with the physical forces that surround him. The bird is 'drawn', apparently phototropically, by the 'dawn', while the smoothly flowing sequence 'his riding | Of the rolling level underneath him steady air' describes two counterpoised forces, that of the air and the bird's intuitive physical responsiveness to it, a relation that is rendered formally in the words 'riding' and 'rolling' as they are balanced on either side of the line break and the large pivotal 'O' of the preposition 'Of'. From this fluent level line the bird moves upwards, 'striding | High', where it comes to a static equipoise, 'then off, off forth on swing', a movement that is likened to the smooth arc of 'a skate's heel . . . on a bow-bend'. The objectivity and the geometrical shapes and relations with which the bird's line of flight is described suggest an abstract scientific diagram. The octave unfolds an elegant epiphany in which the flow of words matches the fluidity of the bird's movement and the currents of air that it responds to with such poise and grace.

This sustained line of poetry and of flight records the resultants of a series of dynamic tensions between the bird and the air, which are likened to a rider and his horse: 'how he rung upon the rein of a wimpling wing'. As was observed earlier of 'Duns Scotus's Oxford', Hopkins emphasizes the physicality of air, often presenting it as analogous to water currents, as, for instance, in his references elsewhere to 'the burl of the fountains of air' (*P.* 28, st. 16) and, more comprehensively, 'air's fine flood' (*P.* 60, l. 51). This analogy is extended in a journal entry that notes cases in which air and water currents become registered in more substantive media: 'a floating flag is like wind visible and what weeds are in a current; it gives it thew and fires it and bloods it in' (*J.* 233). Hopkins's description of the wind as a horse in 'The Windhover' similarly 'gives it thew'; it attributes the air currents with the control and strength of disciplined musculature, effectively describing it as 'a stallion stalwart' (*P.* 38), and so matches it to the bird/rider. Hopkins makes a similar analogy between such fluid force and the muscular form of the horse in a journal entry from 1874: '[I] caught that inscape in the horse that you see in the . . . basreliefs of the Parthenon . . . running on the likeness of a horse to a breaker, a wave of the sea curling over' (*J.* 241–2). The relationship between the bird and the air currents draws together two precisely counterpoised physical forces – 'the hurl and gliding | Rebuffed the big wind' – which, balanced here on either side of the line break, are drawn together in accordance with Hopkins's distinctive formal principle of instress, of 'the flush and foredrawn', as a literally dynamic unity.

The octave of 'The Windhover' shows that the apprehension of form in nature does not simply depend upon the mind, as Hopkins worries it might do in such early poems as 'It was a hard thing to undo this knot', but rather is inherent to the event itself. Form is sunk in the objective relations of the world, here as a physical tension, an instress comprising the dynamically poised relations of the bird and the air. This graceful physical relation correspondingly affects the perceiver viscerally: 'My heart in hiding | Stirred for a bird – the achieve of, the mastery of the thing!' Elsewhere Hopkins describes his experience of his body 'swayed as a piece by the nervous and muscular instress' (*J.* 238), and in this poem the physical tension and poise that define the event he witnesses register in his body directly as a physical stress, a stirring of the heart. Furthermore, the poetry of the octave encourages in the reader a sympathetic experience of this affective instress. The long sentence describing the bird barely allows its reader to pause for breath as it runs its terms together in breathless awe and excitement for six and a half lines. By the time we reach the final part of the octave we too by degrees share in the breathlessness that accompanies the stirring of the poet's heart and expresses itself directly in the last gasping words of the octave: '– the achieve of, the mastery of the thing!'

Broken into tercets, the sestet is, after the flow of the octave's long gliding line, abrupt and conclusive. The event described by the first stanza reaches a crisis here, its dynamism intensified until it catches fire:

> Brute beauty and valour and act, oh, air, pride, plume, here
>   Buckle! AND the fire that breaks from thee then, a billion
> Times told lovelier, more dangerous, O my chevalier!
>
>   No wonder of it: shéer plód makes plough down sillion
> Shine, and blue-bleak embers, ah my dear,
>   Fall, gall themselves, and gash gold-vermilion.

All of the attributes listed in the first line of the sestet are gathered up and caught, first of all in the simultaneity that the final attribute of the line, 'here', confers upon all its predecessors, and then in the fire that results as they 'Buckle!' This line recapitulates the octave's description of the scene by running its attributes together, first of all spaced by the connective 'and', then, after the exclamatory 'oh', simply juxtaposed. The attributes listed at the end of the line are piled one upon the other; the full force of their stresses no longer diluted and slowed by the connective, they enact the pressures that would cause them to 'Buckle!' The impact of the word

'Buckle!' comes partly from its position at the start of a new line. While we read the first line with the benefit of peripheral vision, so that our eyes not only focus on particular words but concurrently read those before and after them, we come at this first word of the second line having been unable to anticipate it in this way. It accordingly comes as a surprise that is enhanced by its plosive consonants and exclamation mark. It marks an abrupt break with the first line, which, as was mentioned earlier, itself recapitulates the rapid run-on lines of the octave that describe the bird's flight. Here, all of a sudden, this line of flight either comes together like a buckled belt or else takes a nose dive: 'Buckle!'

For all its impact, the resolute vertical line and full stop of the exclamation mark after 'Buckle' does not mark the end of the sestet's first sentence. The connective 'and' that was abandoned halfway through the first line is restored here. Imperative and monumental in its capital letters, it formally prepares us for the solemn heart of the epiphany, 'the fire that breaks' from the bird. Of course it also marks a causal link between the dramatic 'Buckle!' and this fire. Norman MacKenzie has suggested that this buckling draws together the bird's attributes in the manner of a completed electrical circuit, an image that makes the resulting fire more literally explicable.[1] Another word for a buckle in this sense is a 'catch', and it works well to sum up the way in which all the terms of the scene come together as an epiphanic event. In this reading the sestet simply brings into clearer focus the epiphany of the octave. Alternatively, the word 'Buckle!' marks the collapse of all the attributes listed in the first line of the sestet and the line of flight traced in the octave, a reading that is corroborated by the poem's final image of the embers falling against one another and catching fire.

Whether the word 'Buckle!' refers to a drawing-together or a collapse of the bird's being, it entails the dissolution of difference in the dynamic unity of fire. This fire is judged, in relation either to the bird in the first stanza or to the actual light reflected off the diving bird, to be 'a billion | Times told lovelier, more dangerous'. It can be usefully compared to another sonnet that has also been dated to 1877 and that begins with another bird catching fire: 'As kingfishers catch fire, dragonflies draw flame' (*P*. 57). The metallic bright blue sheen of the kingfisher's wings catches the light as it darts about in the sun, much as we might also expect (albeit less spectacularly) of the windhover in the octave, which is characterized by its relation to light as the 'king | dom of daylight's dauphin'. The Windhover of the sestet similarly catches fire as it hurls itself downwards, allowing the poise it earlier exerted against the air currents to collapse. In the case of the kingfisher, which is representative for the Windhover of the octave, a highlight is thrown on the bird as it expresses its created nature, 'goes itself', while, from the Windhover's buckling in the sestet, his giving way to pressure or stress, a 'fire breaks' that 'a billion | Times told lovelier' tells directly of Christ's created nature, the infinite splendour of his sacrifice, of the fall he took to redeem fallen man. The embers at the close of the poem 'gash gold-vermilion' in an image that suggests the wounds of the crucified Christ.

Although its critics have consistently identified the Windhover with Christ, the poem itself makes no direct reference to having 'glean[ed] our Saviour' from nature in the manner of 'Hurrahing in Harvest'. Indeed, the only explicit reference it makes to him is its dedication *'To Christ our Lord'*. While this may suggest the poet-persona's dedication to finding Christ in such natural phenomena as the windhover of the title, the main cue for the dominant reading of the poem is the fire that breaks from the bird in the sestet. The reading of this epiphany as Christ breaking like fire from finite nature is consistent with Hopkins's maxim at the start of 'God's Grandeur', which dates from March 1877, about two months before 'The Windhover': 'The world is charged with the grandeur of God. | It will flame out, like shining from shook foil' (*P*. 31). Hopkins's natural theology treats nature as a text, the Book of Nature that tells of its author. The poet accordingly interprets the signs that the world presents to him, but does not make this interpretation explicit in 'The Windhover'. An instress of Christ is 'caught' by Hopkins in the incarnational medium of language, remaining immanent to the poem and waiting to be rediscovered by the reader. 'The Windhover' accordingly encourages its reader to replicate the poet-persona's experience here by finding such immanent meaning, not in the Book of Nature (as the poet did) but in its proxy, the poem.

As well as the imagery of the falling bird and embers that were earlier interpreted as allegories of the Crucifixion, the poet's addressing of the Windhover as 'my chevalier' and the earlier chivalric analogy of the rider suggest that the bird has the status of 'Lord'. As such it corroborates his more specific identification as 'daylight's dauphin', the son of the Sun-King, God the Father. Parallel to this, the possessive 'morning's minion' also suggests this relation of the Father to the Son.[2] Furthermore, the tautologous and repetitive pattern of the phrase 'morning morning's minion' suggests the peculiar relation of sameness and difference that describes the Trinity. The initial reference to 'this morning' can be accordingly referred to the Holy Ghost, an identification that is made at the close of 'God's Grandeur': 'Oh, morning, at the brown brink eastward, springs – | Because the Holy Ghost over the bent | World broods with warm breast and with ah! bright wings' (*P*. 31). The qualities of the fire itself, massive in scale and described as both lovely and 'dangerous', suggest the *sublime*, an apprehension that exceeds our powers to imagine or understand it and that is usually seen to indicate a transcendent principle of being.

The immanent fact of Christ's being suddenly leaps out from the poem once the reader has interpreted its clues and solved the mystery of the fire. In this way the reader may be said independently to discover Christ, instress his Being. By making him immanent to the poem in this way, rather than overt (as in 'Hurrahing in Harvest'), 'The Windhover' functions evangelically to encourage a personal acknowledgement by the reader of Christ, the 'Miracle-in-Mary-of-flame' (*P*. 28, st. 34), and indeed to catch fire in accordance with the pattern of spiritual ascension that the poet's heart traces in 'The Wreck of the *Deutschland*': 'To flash from the flame to the flame' (*P*. 28, st. 3). But what we discover in the sestet is quite different from that which we learn from the octave. The fire that erupts in the sestet appeals to faith, it does not offer direct knowledge. In contrast to the octave, which describes the Windhover with the careful precision of the nature observations in the journals, the sestet provides no such information and shatters any hope of finally consigning this natural phenomenon to the poet's 'treasury of explored beauty', of catching and keeping it.

The fire is symbolic for the deep instress of Christ that the bird yields and the observer receives at this moment, while its magnitude indicates that it dazzles and so defies the sense of sight required for the kind of observations that are made in the first stanza. The 'dangerous' fire that is thrown at the poet and the reader suggests the 'blear and blinding ball' of the Sun, which in 'The Blessed Virgin compared to the Air we Breathe' is identified with God, 'Whose glory bare would blind' (*P.* 60, l. 108). Mercifully, however, this harsh light is 'Sifted to suit our sight' (*P.* 60, 1. 113), diffused by the cooling blue atmosphere that in this poem represents the mediatrix Mary. The morning light that in 'The Windhover' plays on the bird and facilitates the poet's detailed description of it in the octave is like that mediated by Mary, or the mild fire that the kingfishers catch (*P.* 57) and the gentle 'shining from shook foil' in 'God's Grandeur' (*P.* 31) – well suited to human powers of perception. Such cases are emblematic of inscape, in which the infinite flushness of divine stress is 'foredrawn', made finite. However, the sublime fire that erupts in the sestet, a 'billion times' greater than the morning light that illuminates the bird in the first stanza, cannot be 'caught' in this way. A bird of prey, the Windhover is after all an unlikely captive (especially at the moment when it is diving for its prey). The natural phenomenon that is grasped in the octave of 'The Windhover' escapes in the sestet, where it tells of a Being that ultimately transcends human capacities to understand it. At this sublime moment human powers of perception and understanding, represented in the first line of the sestet by the summary list of attributes that the poet has abstracted from his experience of the bird, may also be said to 'Buckle!' The knowledge that nature offers is, as 'The Windhover' dramatizes, ultimately eclipsed by faith, for it surpasses our finite capacities for understanding. This recognition does not mean that Hopkins is a mystic, but simply that he respects the mystery that infinite Being must have for finite being: 'Since, tho' he is under the world's splendour and wonder, | His mystery must be instressed, stressed' (*P.* 28, st. 5).

6

Living with God

'The Windhover' literally highlights the sheer dynamism of stress, both as it inheres in the instress, the tense equilibrium of the 'flush and the foredrawn' that upholds an inscape, which the octave explores, and more radically in the unconditioned and original form of divine being, the fire of pure stress, which the sestet presents. With the contained being of the bird flashing back to its source in God, the poem graphically illustrates the instability of inscape, its paradoxical nature as the finite form of infinite being, a 'piece of being' (*P*. 50). This presents the persona with a sublime experience, as he enjoys in safety an exhilarating terror at the prospect of the fire's overwhelming cosmic energy, 'a billion | Times told lovelier, more dangerous . . .'. He is in the luxurious position of being the beholder rather than his object, the creature whose finite being he perceives to be dissolving here. But he and his fellows also share this paradoxical nature. Indeed, if the Windhover embodies this dynamic being, how much more so does humankind, which is made in God's image? Furthermore, as 'Ribblesdale' makes clear, human beings differ from the rest of nature, 'That canst but only be' (*P*. 58), by being possessed of self-consciousness, so that, unique amongst all beings, we can experience the radical instability of our own selfhood. This chapter examines the reciprocal relations of the human self to its source and sustenance in the Being of God, by looking first of all at man's dependence upon divine stress and then at how we can respond to it.

The first and longest of Hopkins's mature poems, 'The Wreck of the *Deutschland*', begins with an invocation to God in which the poet describes his own creation:

Thou has bound bones and veins in me, fastened me flesh,
And after it almost unmade, what with dread,
Thy doing: and dost they touch me afresh?
Over again I feel they finger and find thee.

(*P.* 28, st. 1)

The moment of creation brings the parts of the body into unity and life, but with it comes original sin, so that consciousness brings dread of God's power and wrath. Such radically riven being needs to be sustained by the stress of God's grace, which is delicately imaged here as the pressure of the Father's finger upon the poet. This idea is elaborated upon a few stanzas later in the analogy cited earlier, where the poet likens his being to a well that is 'roped with, always, . . . | . . . a vein | Of the gospel proffer, a pressure, a principle, Christ's gift' (*P.* 28, st. 4). An unfinished poem, which probably dates from late 1885, begins its account of the poet's relation to divine being with a similar hydrodynamic metaphor:

Thee, God, I come from, to thee go,
All dáy long I like fountain flow
From thy hand out, swayed about
Mote-like in thy mighty glow.

(*P.* 155)

The poet's instress is summed up by the pattern that water forms as, impelled upwards, it meets its equal and opposing force of gravity and so arrives at the dynamic equilibrium of the fountainhead. This is an instance of what Hopkins refers to in his notes 'On Personality, Grace and Free Will' as the ' "burl" of being' (*S.* 154). A burl is a gentle spring or fountain, and the word is also used by analogy for a knot in the grain of wood or in the weave of some fabric. Drawing upon these phenomena, in which a coherent and individuated form emerges from an even and undifferentiated substance, Hopkins's metaphor describes the relation of instress to the universal field of stress. The burl is full and round, like Parmenides' sphere of Being. He refers in his journals to 'the burling and roundness of the world' (*J.* 251). It is, however, also fundamentally unstable, as the reference cited earlier to 'the burl of the fountains of air' (*P.* 28, st. 16) serves to highlight, for these intense currents come from and dissolve into their ground, thin air. The precarious forms of the burl are maintained paradoxically through the fluctuous, flushing nature of their media, their air or water.

This instability is brought out further in the notes on 'Personality, Grace and Free Will', where Hopkins explains that each such burl consists of 'countless cleaves', 'which each of his creatures shews to God's eyes alone' (*S.* 154). Hopkins makes a noun of the verb 'cleave', an odd word that denotes two perfectly contradictory meanings. According to the *OED*, one sense of 'cleave' means to 'To part or divide by a cutting blow; to hew asunder; to split', especially along the grain of wood, a meaning that ties in with one use of the word 'burl'. In this application Hopkins's word suggests that each creature is in God's eyes potentially or actually riven, like the self that is described as 'almost unmade' in 'The Wreck of the *Deutschland*'. However, 'cleave' also means, as the *OED* puts it, 'To stick fast or adhere, as by a glutinous surface', a meaning that suggests liquid cohesion, such as that of the olive oil in 'God's Grandeur' discussed in Chapter 4. This 'foredrawn' quality is the force that holds being together, which Hopkins's notes specify as the stress of grace. Such cleaves are points at which God can see that 'the creature has consented, does consent, to God's will' (*S.* 154). This type of coherence ties in with the extended senses that the *OED* gives this meaning of 'cleave', 'to remain attached, devoted, or faithful' and to 'Stand fast, abide, continue'. More generally, cleaves are for Hopkins points at which God recognizes particular possibilities within the potential of individual selfhood, the burl of being, where this being can either fall apart or draw together more completely and even elevate itself, according to how it responds to the pressure of divine grace. As in 'The Wreck of the *Deutschland*', this pressure is described throughout the notes as the touch of God's finger, so that, for instance, 'elevating' grace 'lifts the receiver from one cleave of being to another and to a vital act in Christ: this is truly God's finger touching the very vein of personality, which nothing else can reach' (*S.* 158).

The '"burl" of being' develops Hopkins's fundamental principle of instress to explain more fully its interactions with the stress of grace. The peculiarly ambivalent 'cleave', like the word 'Buckle' in 'The Windhover', focuses in one word the dramatic tension between dispersal and coherence that defines for Hopkins finite instances of being. The stress that upholds their being, in the metaphors of the well, the fountain, and the burl, is transient, their form at once constant and constantly dissipating. So, while the first line of the poem, 'Thee, God, I come from, to thee go', seems on the face of it to refer simply to the birth and death of the poet, with the metaphor of the fountain in the second line it becomes clear that the flow of the poet's being comes from and goes to God ceaselessly, 'All dáy long'. In the third line, however, we learn that this occurs at the discretion of God's hand, which pours forth this grace, this stress of being.

The poet's being flows 'From thy hand out, swayed about | Mote-like in thy mighty glow'. The ambiguous motion that proceeds from God's hand at once recalls the characterization, familiar from the journals, of the dynamic unity of instress and inscape as swerved and swayed, but it also suggests a troubling or destablizing of the flow of being, the threat of its dispersion and dissolution. It recalls the mighty 'sway of the sea' in 'The Wreck of the *Deutschland*' (*P.* 28, st. 1), and the human beings who fall prey to it, such as the strong sailor who, having tied himself by a rope to the rigging and been 'pitched to his death at a blow', is then 'dandled the two and fro' (*P.* 28, st. 16). The poem meditates upon the massive force and mystery of God, whose Being is expressed in the might of ocean and storm and apparently allows the death at sea of the *Deutschland*'s passengers, a group of German Catholic nuns fleeing persecution in their homeland. The poem reminds us, as we have seen from its first stanza, that human selfhood is always on the verge of its unmaking by God's sublime power. The later unfinished poem depicts the self in similarly paradoxical terms as a sustained transitory moment between coming from and returning to its source in God. The 'flow' of the poet's being is accordingly understood in this later poem as infinitely diminutive and vulnerable to God's awesome being, like a speck of dust floating in the beams of the sun ('such a nothing is the creature before its creator' (*S.* 155)). Understanding his relation to God in such terms, Hopkins accordingly describes it tentatively in both poems as humble and courteous – in 'The Wreck': 'For I greet him the days I meet him, and bless when I understand' (*P.* 28, st. 5), and in the later poem:

> What I know of thee I bless,
> As acknowledging thy stress
> On my being and as seeing
> Something of thy holiness.
>
> (*P.* 155)

The first stanza of 'Thee, God, I come from' describes God's stress as it defines and upholds the poet's being, and the second stanza, quoted here, the poet's balancing 'counter-stress' (*S.* 158) of recognition and appreciation. This reciprocal relation of 'stress' and 'counter-stress' is the form for Hopkins's protocols of catching, greeting, and blessing. Another of his analogies for such interactions, that of the echo, allows him to explore a range of human responses to divine stress, for echoes represent their original sound with varying degrees of accuracy, from a crisp clear repetition to an unmeaning dissipated noise, like that suggested by the early poem 'My prayers must meet a brazen heaven|And fail or scatter all away' (*P.* 18). As we know from 'Duns Scotus's Oxford', Hopkins understands sound as a physical stress that is transmitted through the medium of the air. Similarly, in the poem 'Spring', the sound of the thrush's song is rendered substantive and energetic as it bounces in echoes off the trees and hits the ear like gushing water or atmospheric electricity: 'and thrush|Through the echoing timber does so rinse and wring | The ear, its strikes like lightnings to hear him sing' (*P.* 33). This liquid metaphor is used also in an unfinished poem, in which 'The whole landscape flushes on a sudden at a sound' (*P.* 146). Building upon this understanding of sound, Hopkins uses the echo as an analogy for individual responsiveness to the grace of mortal or physical beauty in his 1882 poem 'The Leaden Echo and the Golden Echo' (*P.* 59).

This long poem consists of two parts, 'The Leaden Echo' and 'The Golden Echo', which offer complementary understandings of mortal beauty, echoes of an absolute truth. The echo here is an auditory analogy to Plato's shadows in his allegory of the cave,[1] a phenomenal reflection of a pure form or absolute truth and our only access to this original. The echoes are distinguished by the quality of their media, the lead or gold that receives and returns the original sound. The lead is a dull and opaque conductor of sound, while the gold offers sharp and accurate reflection, an undistorted echo of the original signal. Put another way, the Leaden Echo is the narcissistic reflection of the mirror, the Golden Echo a meditative reflection that situates and celebrates mortal beauty in the context of Hopkins's Christian cosmology. While the poem could be read as being spoken in one voice, the strongly contrastive nature of the attitudes expressed in each part suggests that the lead and the gold should be treated as separate personae.

'The Leaden Echo' begins by asking 'How to kéep – is there ány, is there none such, nowhere known some, bow or brooch or braid or brace, láce, latch or catch or key to keep | Back beauty, keep it, beauty, beauty, beauty ... from vanishing away?' The jerky movement of the syntax here, as the speaker dashes about desperately trying to gain some assurance that mortal beauty can be preserved, indicates that in being reflected by the lead an original clear sound has become a fragmented and confused echo. The dead weight of egoism makes the echo leaden, prevents it from freely resonating outwards in the manner of the Golden Echo. The pause after the repeated word 'beauty' demonstrates the speaker's reluctance to face the possibility of it 'vanishing away', but, the more this possibility is dwelt upon, the more convincing it becomes for him, so that he answers his original question about ways of keeping beauty in unequivocal terms: 'No there's none, there's none, O no there's none.' While the speaker's shrunken hopes and resignation register in a series of relatively brief lines, a further line gathers in overweeningly disproportionate length as visions of mortality take hold of the imagination: 'Age and age's evils, hoar hair, | Ruck and wrinkle, drooping, dying, death's worst, winding sheets, tombs and worms and tumbling to decay.' Nothing is fixed here, as through the masterly use of assonance and alliteration word sounds mutate chromatically one into the next so that they replicate the helpless tumbling motion they ascribe to the process of physical decline. As 'The Leaden Echo' comes to its close, the early insistent repetition of the word 'beauty' is paralleled and superseded by other repeated words, the dull negations 'none' and 'no' and then 'despair'. These leaden echoes are promptly answered by 'The Golden Echo':

> O there's none; no no no there's none:
> Be beginning to despair, to despair,
> Despair, despair, despair, despair.
>
> THE GOLDEN ECHO
>
> Spare!
>
> There ís one . . .

This turn follows the classical echo poem in the retort it makes to the indulgently repetitious 'despair' of a single (indeed spare!) 'Spare!' 'The Golden Echo' is not a direct echo of 'The Leaden Echo' but a corrective to it, a precise echo of the transcendent truth of mortal beauty available through Christian belief. It is indeed in every sense the more *faithful* echo. 'The Golden Echo' suggests that the leaden echoes of 'none' and 'despair' are distortions of 'one' and 'Spare!', of the truth of the one God who spares mortal beauty and keeps it 'with fonder a care'. The Leaden Echo's negative trinities of 'no' (l. 14) and 'none' (l. 5) are answered by the positive 'one'. Rather than the hopelessness of 'none', we are offered a 'one' that rhymes with 'sun', its synaesthetic golden echo that suggests the equation of the One of God with the sun that was introduced in Chapter 5's discussion of 'The Windhover' and 'The Blessed Virgin compared to the Air we Breathe'. The downcast word sound 'Despair' is shorn of its negative prefix and made active and imperative through its exclamation mark; 'Spare!'

The pivotal word 'Spare!' is, as W. H. Gardner observes, like a change of musical key marking the transition to 'The Golden Echo',[2] and indeed it functions as the key note from which several important rhymes, like a series of tonal variants, align and highlight its truth: the 'there!' 'where' mortal beauty is 'kept with fonder a care' by God. This last phrase, the final reassuring answer to the anxious question that opens 'The Leaden Echo', rolls through the poem's last lines in slightly varied forms. It is dwelt upon, savoured, and celebrated, for here we have a 'care' for mortal beauty that is 'fonder' than the obsessive narcissistic concern of 'The Leaden Echo', the implication being that God cares more for mortal beauty than do the individuals who embody it. The word 'fonder' is accordingly brought to the fore here, providing the first term of the poem's final rhyme. Indeed, the peculiar musicality of 'The Golden Echo' can be traced to its source through the word sound 'fonder', which after its last occurrence moderates alliteratively into the directive 'follow' while the rest of the word is taken up by its rhyme 'yonder'. The word 'yonder' is repeated in the final lines as a series of gentle reverberations, which gesture towards the transcendent origin of the Golden Echo, the pure note in which all true beauty has its source and expression: 'back to God, beauty's self and beauty's giver'. The poem returns to the Pythagorean conceit of the early poem 'Let me be to Thee as the circling bird', which describes God as the 'dominant' note. Here, however, as we have begun to observe, such Pythagoreanism is entrenched more completely in the patterns of the verse. 'The Leaden Echo and the Golden Echo' was written as a song for a play that Hopkins began composing on St Winefred's Well, and indeed he says of the poem in a letter to Dixon that 'I never did anything more musical' (*L2* 149).

The longer patterned lines of 'The Golden Echo' are, as befits the Pythagorean order of the cosmology that they acknowledge, more harmonious and balanced in their music than 'The Leaden Echo':

> Come then, your ways and airs and looks, locks, maidengear, gallantry and gaiety and grace,
> Winning ways, airs innocent, maiden manners, sweet looks, loose locks, long locks, lovelocks, gaygear, going gallant, girlgrace –
> Resign them, sign them, seal them, send them, motion them with breath,
> And with sighs soaring, soaring sîghs, deliver
> Them; beauty-in-the-ghost, deliver it, early now, long before death
> Give beauty back, beauty, beauty, beauty, back to God, beauty's self and beauty's giver.

The metre in this central passage of 'The Golden Echo' is more regular than in 'The Leaden Echo': 'Wînning wáys, airs înnocent, máiden mánners, swéet looks, lóose locks, lóng locks, lóvelocks, gáygear, góing gállant, gírlgrace.' Such even rhythms and gently modulated scales of alliteration and assonance endow the vision of 'The Golden Echo' with an underlying Pythagorean order and stability that correlates with a God 'whose beauty is', in the words of 'Pied Beauty', 'past change' (*P*. 37).

The form of the Golden Echo, which so perfectly reflects the Christian doctrine that the poem endorses, is that of scrupulous correspondence and balance. Indeed, 'The Golden Echo' draws 'The Leaden Echo' into such relations by directly addressing its terms. The plea to keep the gifts, retain the graces, of mortal beauty that impels 'The Leaden Echo' 'to keep | Back beauty, keep it, beauty, beauty, beauty' is answered by 'The Golden Echo' as it urges us to 'Give beauty back, beauty, beauty, beauty, back to God, beauty's self and beauty's giver'. But, while this line from the second part of the poem offers a formal echo of the first, its internal form is more balanced, for the Golden Echo marks the 'counter-stress' that responds precisely and self-consciously to the original 'stress' of grace: 'Give beauty . . . back to . . . beauty's giver.' Such formal mirroring of phrases emblematizes the Golden Echo: 'sighs soaring, soaring síghs'.

The Golden Echo gives beauty back to its giver with an exacting reciprocity that is described and explained more fully by the sestet of 'As kingfishers catch fire':

> Í say more: the just man justices;
> Keeps gráce: thát keeps all his goings graces;
> Acts in God's eye what in God's eye he is –
> Chríst. For Christ plays in ten thousand places,
> Lovely in limbs, and lovely in eyes not his
> To the Father through the features of men's faces.
>
> (*P*. 57)

Like the personae identified with lead and gold in the 'Echo' poem, human beings in the 'kingfishers' sonnet are the media that receive and return divine grace: the beauty of Christ 'plays' 'To the Father *through* the features of men's faces' (emphasis added). The limbs and facial features express Christ's beauty, indeed so much so that the poem presents them as inextricable from one another in a manner that is glossed by the notes 'On Personality, Grace and Free Will': 'It is as if a man said: That is Christ playing at me and me playing at Christ, only that is no play but truth; That is Christ *being me* and me being Christ' (*S.* 154). This makes explicit the implication of the 'Echo' poem, that mortal beauty is divine beauty incarnate, the beauty of Christ (and as such can be kept permanently only by God). It exemplifies Hopkins's dictum in 'To what serves Mortal Beauty?', that 'Self flashes off frame and face' (*P.* 62). Physical beauty is inner grace, the beautiful character, made manifest; 'as we Aristotelian Catholics say . . . the soul is the form of the body' (*L1* 95). But such beauty is not passive (it does not just look good), for it 'flashes' off the body and face, like the various forms of fire, 'shining', and lightning that are familiar from 'The Windhover', 'God's Grandeur', and 'As kingfishers catch fire'. Such imagery refers to the way in which a creature's physical actions literally highlight, *actualize*, its essential nature. In the sestet of the 'kingfishers' poem beauty is presented accordingly as moral action, the play of 'lovely' human 'limbs' and 'eyes' that occurs as 'the just man justices'. Justice here is synonymous with keeping grace – that is, with instressing grace, with acknowledging it and acting through it; 'thát keeps all his goings graces'. It is through such moral action, the exercise of limbs and eyes to reciprocate 'God's better beauty, grace' (*P.* 62), that human beings can give beauty back to God, as 'The Golden Echo' urges, 'early now, long before death'.

The sestet of 'As kingfishers catch fire' explains that human being flourishes as the willing medium through which 'Christ plays' – through which divine stress flows freely in the manner described by the unfinished poem 'Thee, God, I come from, to thee go, | All dáy long I like fountain flow'. While the metaphor of the well in 'The Wreck of the *Deutschland*' depicts selfhood as sustained by the flow of divine stress or grace, 'a pressure, a principle, Christ's gift', 'The Leaden Echo and the Golden Echo' emphasizes the reciprocal principle, the gifts of being that the human self can make to God. Here, as in the 'kingfishers' poem, the model for such giving is Christ's sacrifice. The moral text that the 'Echo' poem elaborates is drawn from the Christlike example of St Winefred's martyrdom. A young Welsh noblewoman living in the seventh century, St Winefred is said to have provoked the lust of prince

Caradoc, but having dedicated her virginity to God she 'died in defence of her chastity' (*L1* 40), decapitated by his sword. St Winefred acquiesces completely to grace: 'For grace is any action, activity, on God's part by which, in creating or after creating, he carries the creature to or towards the end of its being, which is its selfsacrifice to God and its salvation' (*S.* 154). At the place that her head came to rest, so the legend goes, her uncle St Beuno miraculously restored her to life and called into being the spring, which, 'favouring virgin freshness yet' (*P.* 139), bears her name. By surrendering her life to God completely Winefred is given new life and salvation, not only through physical resurrection but as a principle of divine grace that acts through the stress of the spring and its miraculous curative powers, which Hopkins found so affecting:

> The strong unfailing flow of the water and the chain of cures from year to year all these centuries took hold of my mind with wonder at the bounty of God in one of His saints, the sensible thing so naturally and gracefully uttering the spiritual reason of its being (which is all in true keeping with the story of St Winefred's death and recovery) and the spring in place leading back the thoughts by its spring in time to its spring in eternity: even now the stress and buoyancy and abundance of the water is before my eyes. (*J.* 261)

By giving her beauty back to God so completely, St Winefred is transformed into divine stress simple and incarnate.

The phenomenon of St Winefred's Well, like those of the burl and the fountain that probably derive from it, and indeed Hopkins's entire ontology of stress, draws together physical with spiritual properties. Similarly, the two complementary attitudes to mortal beauty, to the gift of embodied human being, that 'The Leaden Echo and the Golden Echo' elaborates are presented as separate substances. They are each punningly identified with metal or *mettle,* the stuff of a particular character. The analogy that the poem draws between character and the properties of material media is comparable to that in 'The Handsome Heart: at a Gracious Answer' (*P.* 47). The child, the Handsome Heart of the title, having been asked what gift he would most like the poet to buy him, replies 'Father, what you buy me I like best', and then, when asked again, he reiterates his answer: 'still plied and pressed, | He swung to his first poised purport of reply'. 'The Handsome Heart' is in this image compared to an iron compass needle. This and the metallic analogies of the 'Echo' poem suggest that Hopkins regards character as a substance that is both malleable and fixed and enduring. He follows the broadly Aristotelian principle that character is formed and fixed as we become habituated to virtue or vice through our actions (*'What I do is me'* (*P*. 57)), but he adds that we have a freedom of play in the way we act and form this character, which can if we are open to it be influenced by divine grace. The compass analogy is elaborated upon in the notes 'On Personality, Grace and Free Will' to explain free will and its interactions with grace: 'The will is surrounded by the objects of desire as the needle by the points of the compass. It has play then in two dimensions' (*S*. 157), which is to say that it is free to move in an arc to any of its desires. The stress of grace is in the compass analogy identified with the stress of polar magnetism, 'stimulating its action, in the right plane and in the right direction, towards the right object' (*S*. 158). The compass needle that the poem identifies with 'The Handsome Heart' is a material substance that can be 'plied and pressed' but, having been subjected to such external pressure, remains true to its nature and exercises its freedom of movement by resuming its alignment with the earth's polar magnetic axis, just as the moral substance of the heart, which is both 'wild and self-instressed', morally independent and self-determined, freely aligns itself with the stress of grace. Of the Leaden Echo and the Golden Echo it is of course the latter that gives the Gracious Answer, urging those possessed of mortal beauty to 'forfeit' it 'freely'.

Parallel to the analogy of the compass needle, which by moving freely comes into alignment with the earth's magnetic field, 'The Leaden Echo and the Golden Echo' sees the metal, the mettle or character, of its speakers to act freely to produce its echo, as each reverberates with different degrees of responsiveness to 'the tenderest truth' of divine grace. These analogies, of metals responding to such external stresses as physical pressure, polar magnetism, and sound vibrations, describe the freedom of will with which particular characters meet external stresses with their own counter-stresses. The relation of substance to sound, the basis for the analogy of the

'Echo' poem, is fundamental to Hopkins's ontology of stress as he develops it from the Pythagorean discovery introduced in Chapter 2, which established that a proportionate relation exists between the length and tautness of a string and the musical note it can produce. He explains free will and the formation, maintenance, and expression of moral character through this analogy. Each being has for Hopkins a particular instress, a tension like that of a tight string, which he describes as a particular 'pitch of being' or 'stress' (*S.* 156). 'Pitch' is a tightening, an elevating of individual stress, but it is also expressive, as it yields a distinctive pitch of sound. In 'The Handsome Heart', for example, the child is 'self-instressed' but nevertheless urged by the poet to 'brace sterner that strain!' (*P.* 47), further to intensify and define his pitch of stress. The analogy of the taut string brings to the fore the expressiveness of such being, for, as the octave of the 'kingfishers' poem puts it, 'each tucked string tells'. Each such being 'Selves – goes itself; *myself* it speaks and spells' (*P.* 57). But only a being 'at stress' can respond in this way to the 'pressure' of grace, the touch of 'God's finger' (*S.* 158).

'*Pitch* is', Hopkins writes, 'ultimately simple positiveness, that by which being differs from and is more than nothing and not-being' (*S.* 151). It is the response, the expressive counter-stress to God's stresses of grace: 'For I greet Him the days that I meet him' (*P.* 28, st. 5). It is the quality of assent, a radical and abiding principle for Hopkins, which can be traced back to the 1868 notes on 'Parmenides', where he writes that 'nothing is so pregnant and straightforward to the truth as simple *yes* and *is*' (*J.* 127). It is the starting point for his belief: 'I did say yes|O at lightning and lashed rod' (*P.* 28, st. 2). Such assent is emphatically active: 'So that this pitch might be expressed, if it were good English, *the doing* be, *the doing* choose, *the doing* so-and-so . . . it is free action, moral action.' It is very much the principle of the active selfhood outlined in the sestet of the 'kingfishers' poem. Here it marks an individual pitch of being that suggests to Hopkins that it is 'the same as Scotus's *ecceitas*' (*S.* 151). The Golden Echo is the complete assent, the full dedication of individual being, of mortal beauty, to God. The metal wholeheartedly responds in kind to the divine stress of sound it receives, just as the finely instressed character expresses its 'pitch of being' under the pressure of divine stress.

While the Golden Echo is sharply focused and undistorting, crisply and faithfully delivering back what is given to it, the Leaden Echo is dull and unresponsive. It selfishly tries to hold on to what is given to it, thereby muffling and perverting its distinctive 'pitch' of created being. The attitude it voices is that of the sinful man described in 'Ribblesdale', another poem from late 1882, who is 'To his own selfbent so bound, so tied to his turn' (*P.* 58). It is an instance of 'balked' (*S.* 137) being, of being that, by turning in on itself and away from God, follows the pattern established by Lucifer: 'This song of Lucifer's was a dwelling on his own beauty, an instressing of his own inscape, and like a performance on the organ and instrument of his own being' (*S.* 200–1). Moreover, this song drew others into it: 'They would not listen to the note which summoned each to his own place (Jude 6.) and distributed them here and there in the liturgy of the sacrifice; they gathered rather closer and closer home under Lucifer's lead and drowned it, raising a countermusic and countertemple and altar, a counterpoint of dissonance and not of harmony' (*S.* 201). These 1881 notes on 'Creation and Redemption: The Great Sacrifice' sum up the basic oppositions of selfishness and sacrifice, and of dissonant music and Pythagorean harmony that respectively inform 'The Leaden Echo' and 'The Golden Echo'. The Leaden Echo punningly follows 'Lucifer's lead'.

In contrast to the Pythagorean harmony and balance of the Golden Echo, the Leaden Echo is 'a counterpoint of dissonance' and its ultimate sin that of despair. And this is indeed the ultimate sin, for, according to Catholic doctrine, despair is the one unforgivable sin, for it is seen to demonstrate a proud presumption that God has no power to help one or does not care, a conviction that 'The Leaden Echo' resonates with but is immediately disproved by 'The Golden Echo' that follows it. It is not mortality but the sin of despair that undermines the pitch of stress, as the opening lines of a later 'sonnet of desolation' make clear: 'Not, I'll not, carrion comfort, Despair, not feast on thee; | Not untwist – slack they may be – these last strands of man | In me . . .' (*P.* 64). These are the very strands that grace brings back to stress, for, as the poem 'The Soldier' puts it, Christ 'of all can reeve a rope best' (*P.* 63), his grace can draw together, instress, the parts of human beings that, as we saw earlier, are from birth 'almost unmade'. Despair, the refusal to acknowledge such grace, marks the irredeemable collapse of the stress that holds the strands of selfhood together in the tight unity of individual instress.

7

Breathing in and Speaking out

The argument of this book began by using the early poem 'Let me be to Thee as the circling bird' to introduce the logic of Hopkins's project, the way in which he strives to draw himself and his experience of the world into harmonious relation with God. The poem outlines a Pythagorean cosmology in which God's 'authentic cadence' resonates in Creation. The poet wishes to be like the bird and the bat, which each produce a 'changeless note', an echo of this Platonic 'authentic cadence'. He does this by finding his 'music in a common word'. The present chapter examines Hopkins's understanding of the word as utterance and object, and the way he theorizes it through his metaphysic of instress and inscape. It argues that this understanding of language is precisely what distinguishes the later poetry, which begins in 1875 with 'The Wreck of the *Deutschland*', from the early poetry, which he abandoned when he joined the Society of Jesus in 1868.

Hopkins comes to recognize the materiality of words through their sounds. As we have seen, he conceives of sound itself as a physical property, first of all through his Pythagoreanism and later through his idea of stress. In 'Let me be to Thee', the pun on the word 'rings' in the description of the 'bat with tender and air-crisping wings | That shapes in half-light his departing rings' depicts this animal, and by implication 'the circling bird', as not only emitting the 'changeless note' but as physically orbiting around it, as embodying its 'rings'. The poet wishes that his self-expressive 'music' and actions would, like those of the bird and the bat, exist in a harmonious relationship with God, an ideal that is as we have seen elaborated more completely and confidently in the sestet of 'As kingfishers catch fire'. 'Let me be to Thee' highlights Hopkins's desire to understand and experience the world as a grand unity, a desire that informs his later metaphysic of stress, instress, and inscape. By building upon the radical physical principle of stress, his doctrine is able fully to theorize the relation between the material reality of Creation and its source and sustenance in God's Being. This mechanistic ontology allows Hopkins to renew the pun he made in 'Let me be to Thee' in the 'kingfishers' poem: 'As tumbled over rim in roundy wells | Stones ring' (*P.* 57). Whereas the early poem in effect choreographs the circular motion of the bat's flight to produce a pun on the acoustic 'rings' of its cries, a rather fanciful or aestheticized relation between the movement and the sound, in the later poem the pun describes a scientifically necessary and objective relation. The outward moving ripples that 'ring' the water furnish a visual parallel to the concentric pattern of the sound waves that 'ring' up from the depth of the well. This relation is grounded in the physics of hydrodynamics and sound, as the parallel concentric rings of the water wavelets and the sound waves are produced as each form of energy meets the resistance of its respective medium – the force of the dropped stone through the water, and the resulting sound through the air.

The pun on the word 'ring' in the 'kingfishers' poem shows the way that sound becomes substance for Hopkins, as it becomes registered in the media of the water and the air. Such reverberating sound of course provides the central metaphor for 'The Leaden Echo and the Golden Echo'. Here, much as in 'Let me be to Thee', the Pythagorean note is found not in music but in words. The 'Echo' poem demonstrates through the substance of the poem, the very words that the Leaden Echo uses to express its despair, that divine grace was always available to it, for the Golden Echo discloses that words of hope are immanent to the leaden words of hopelessness and resignation. As was noted earlier, the Golden Echo draws out positive qualities that are contained within the negative, waiting to be found by the voice of hope; 'Spare!' from 'Despair' and 'one' from 'none'. Lead is transformed here into Gold. A similarly alchemical wordplay closes the poem 'That Nature is a Heraclitean Fire and of the comfort of the

Resurrection', as simple carbon, the ash left from the fluctuous 'bonfire' of nature, is transformed into diamond; mortal man is given everliving life through the Resurrection:

> Across my foundering deck shone
> A beacon, an eternal beam. | Flesh fade, and mortal trash
> Fall to the residuary worm; | world's wildfire, leave but ash:
> In a flash, at a trumpet crash,
> I am all at once what Christ is, | since he was what I am, and
> This Jack, joke, poor potsherd, | patch, matchwood, immortal
> diamond,
> Is immortal diamond.
>
> (*P.* 72)

The verbal transformations in the 'Echo' poem occur as the purging of a leaden dross, the heavy sin of despair. Similarly in the 'Heraclitean Fire' sonnet, 'mortal trash' is reduced by death, the wages of sin (Rom. 5: 12), to 'ash'. However, from this point our being is supplemented, added to, as the words 'flash' and 'crash' supervene upon 'ash'. The 'flash' harks back to 'the fire that breaks from' the Windhover, especially here as it is associated with a 'crash', the apocalyptic 'trumpet crash' that announces the Resurrection. The redeeming work of Christ's Crucifixion is completed in the resurrection of the bodies of the dead (1 Cor. 15: 54–7); the 'flash' that we are familiar with from the fire of 'The Windhover' endures until the end of time as the 'eternal beam' of the Resurrection. Like the 'fire' of 'The Windhover', this 'flash' is an infinite stress. Just as charcoal subjected to intense pressure over geological periods of time becomes diamond, so here the residual ash of carbon-based human being is changed under the infinite pressure of divine stress into eternal life, the frozen fire of the diamond in which the light of God plays endlessly.

The crucial supplement that Christ gives to human beings is rendered most starkly in the formula 'I am, and', which initiates the poem's final rhyme. The most basic assertion of being, 'I am', is supplemented with the simple connective 'and'. The phrase means that 'I am (through Christ and the Resurrection) *more* than myself', a sense that literally crystallizes in its rhyme with 'diamond'. The whole of the poem traces vast patterns of flux, as 'Million-fuelèd, nature's bonfire burns on', and comes in its last lines to focus upon the natural change from human life to death. All of this flux comes to rest with the remarkable final couplet, which restates an idea that is put more clearly in the line before it: 'I am all at once what Christ is, since he was what I am.' Change and its fluctuous word patterns are finally banished by this tautology (and pedantically perfect rhyme), which pivots about the copula, the simple assertion of *being*: 'immortal diamond, | Is immortal diamond'.

The tendency in Hopkins's poems to enact meanings through the physical relations of word sounds, which this book has noted at various points along its way, is one of the most distinctive aspects of his poetry. Chapter 3 introduced this use of language in which, rather than passively representing things, words actively participate in the dynamism of the phenomenal world, in *being*. This was, as his optimistic notes on onomatopoeia indicate, one of Hopkins's earliest hopes for language. The early word lists, which are usually arranged as scales of word sounds, extend the mimetic possibility of onomatapoeia to the relations between words, which the later poetry draws upon and develops so effectively in its bold use of alliteration and assonance. The word lists develop relations between words that are suited to expressing Hopkins's experience of nature at this time, which is also recorded in his early diaries and journals. These observations focus upon change and variety in nature and try to find an underlying form that anchors such flux, while, parallel to this, in the word lists, Hopkins finds order in the flux of language as he draws together words that share the same sound and he attributes to them a shared meaning. As most of the examples cited earlier demonstrate, the alliterative and assonant sequences in the poems, the legacy of the early word lists, lend themselves to depicting such flux and diversity in nature: 'Lét life, wáned, ah lét life wind|Off hér once skéined stained véined variety . . .' (*P*. 61).

Once he has established his metaphysic of instress and inscape, Hopkins is less anxious to find generic form in the flux of nature and to fix it in language. Following Parmenides, he takes the primacy of *being* as the starting point for his metaphysic. This allows him to find form, inscape, in the most individual and apparently aberrant natural phenomena – in

'All things counter, original, spare, strange', for all are grounded in Being, the God 'whose beauty is past change' (*P.* 38). As well as theorizing being in this way, both as individual and as ultimate and all-encompassing, the 'Parmenides' notes also attribute language with the power to acknowledge it: 'The truth in thought is Being, stress, and each word is one way of acknowledging Being' (*J.* 129). As the respective stanzas of 'The Windhover' demonstrate, Hopkins comes to see language as the means of acknowledging both the particularity of the individual being or event ('I caught this morning morning's minion') and Being itself ('the fire that breaks from thee . . .').

Hopkins explores further the relation between language and his idea of being or stress in 'Rhythm and the other structural parts of Rhetoric – verse', the lecture notes he wrote sometime between September 1873 and July 1874 when he was Professor of Rhetoric at Manresa House. As in the 'Parmenides' notes, instances of being are characterized here in terms of mechanical stress. But in these notes it is words themselves that are described as physical objects, as they become embodied, bodied forth, in utterance:

> we speak of the accent of words, that is of syllables; for the accent of a word means its strongest accent, the accent of its best accented syllable. This is of two kinds – that *of pitch* (tonic) and that *of stress* (emphatic). We may think of words as heavy bodies, as indoor or out of door objects of nature or man's art. Now every visible palpable body has a centre of gravity round which it is in balance and a centre of illumination or *highspot* or *quickspot* up to which it is lighted and down from which it is shaded. The centre of gravity is like the accent of stress, the highspot like the accent of pitch, for pitch is like light and colour, stress like weight, and as in some things as air and water the centre of gravity is either unnoticeable or changeable so there may be languages in a fluid state in which there is little difference of weight or stress between syllables or what there is changes and again as it is only glazed bodies that shew the highspot well so there may be languages in which the pitch is unnoticeable.
>
> English is of this kind, the accent of stress strong, that of pitch weak – only they go together for the most part. (*J.* 269)

The way that Hopkins theorizes physical bodies here, as each having 'a centre of gravity round which it is in balance', describes the most simple mechanical instress, the counter-poise of opposing stresses. The poise and unity of the word are described in Hopkins's analogy as proceeding from its metrical stress. No matter how many syllables a word may have, all are drawn together by its stress into the organic unity of a body. The tension between the quantity of syllables and the strength of the metrical stress corrresponds to that between 'the flush and foredrawn', which is to say that the word effectively draws together as an instress. This conception of the spoken word allows Hopkins to refer, in some notes on 'Poetry and Verse' that he also wrote while at Manresa House, to 'the inscape of speech' and to define poetry in terms of it: 'Poetry is in fact speech only employed to carry the inscape of speech for the inscape's sake' (*J.* 289). According to this definition, it is not the content, the meaning, that is important to poetry, but the abstract form of spoken language, the ways in which individual words draw together about their 'centre of gravity' and form patterns, 'the shape which is contemplated for its own sake' (*J.* 289). 'Verse is speech having a marked figure, order of sounds independent of meaning' (*J.* 267). So it is that the meanings of Hopkins's mature poetry are often relatively inaccessible, hidden behind the often elaborate formal relations of word sounds that it brings to the fore. One of the most powerful ways in which form can eclipse denotation in the mature poetry is through the concentrated use of metrical stress that Hopkins refers to as 'sprung rhythm.'

Hopkins's ontology of stress informs his poetry most obviously through sprung rhythm, which he writes 'makes verse stressy'.[1] The basic principle is sketched by Hopkins in the lecture notes on 'Rhetoric', where it is not only the word that gains its unifying 'centre of gravity' from a single stress, but the metrical foot is described by analogy with it: 'The foot is the rhythmic word with its strong beat for emphatic accent' (*J.* 273). 'This then is the essence of sprung rhythm: *one stress makes one foot*, no matter how many or few the syllables' (*L2* 23). Hopkins does not claim to have invented sprung rhythm but only to have developed it, and he finds examples of it in such diverse sources as Shakespeare and children's nursery rhymes. By identifying each metrical foot with its stress, sprung rhythm allows Hopkins a great deal of flexibility: 'in sprung rhythm, the stress being more *of* a stress, being more important, allows of greater variation in the slack and this latter may range from three syllables to none at all – *regularly*, so that paeons (three short syllables and one long or three slack and one stressy) are regular in sprung rhythm, but in common rhythm can occur only by licence' (*L2* 39). Sprung rhythm stresses stress, it facilitates the concentrated 'stressy' effect of such lines as the following from 'The Wreck of the *Deutschland*': 'The sóur scýthe crínge, and the bléar sháre cóme' (*P*. 28, st. 11). Indeed, Hopkins writes that, strictly speaking, it is only such examples as this that are truly sprung: 'I sh[oul]d add that the word Sprung which I use for this rhythm means something like *abrupt* and applies by rights only where one stress follows another running, without syllable between' (*L2* 23).

In an account he gives to Dixon of the poem's composition, Hopkins writes that, while 'The Wreck of the *Deutschland*' is the first of his poems fully to employ sprung rhythm, it was not for him a new discovery at the time he wrote the poem: 'I had long had haunting my ear the echo of a new rhythm which now I realised on paper' (*L2* 14). Hopkins first experiments with sprung rhythm a few months after he formulates his doctrine of stress in the 'Parmenides' notes. In a letter to Bridges dated 7 August 1868 he encloses a revised version of some poetry for a play he had begun writing on St. Dorothea. The letter refers to 'the peculiar beat I have introduced into St. Dorothea', which he indicates and accentuates in the accompanying draft by the addition of stress marks (*PW* 42c). Hopkins makes it clear in this letter that his 'peculiar beat' marked for him a departure from his earlier poetry, for, while he includes his new version of 'Lines for a Picture of St. Dorothea' and commends it as a new 'development' in prosody, he also writes that he has destroyed the earlier work: 'I cannot send my *Summa* for it is burnt with my other verses: I saw they w[oul]d interfere with my state and vocation' (*L1* 24). The implication here is that, unlike his earlier poetic practice, the new 'development' by which he accentuates metrical stress is consistent with his religious vocation.

There are at most only a couple of months separating Hopkins's 'Parmenides' notes from a series of momentous journal entries he wrote in early May 1868, which record that he 'Resolved to be a religious', to destroy his early verse (in an act he refers to as the 'Slaughter of the innocents'), and to write no more poetry (*J.* 164–5). The theocentric metaphysic of stress that Hopkins establishes in the 'Parmenides' notes clarifies his understanding of Being, and the grounds of his religious belief. It is likely that these private meditations not only quickened his sense of vocation but also led him to reject his early poetic practice in favour of experiments with sprung rhythm, which were limited at this time to a few versions of the 'St Dorothea' poem. The lecture notes on 'Rhetoric' and 'Poetry and Verse' show that, in the period between writing the 'Parmenides' notes and 'The Wreck of the *Deutschland*', Hopkins not only develops a particular interest in metrical stress, but also theorizes it in terms of physical stress and inscape. He evidently worked during this time to overcome the clash he perceived between the vocations of priest and poet, so that, when one of his superiors suggested to him in December 1875 that someone should write a poem on the *Deutschland* disaster, Hopkins was able not only to begin writing immediately in one of the most distinctive voices in English poetry, but to do so in a poem that is by far his longest.

The 'Parmenides' notes provide Hopkins with the grounds to develop a practice of poetry that is integral (rather than inimical) to his religious life. By establishing that 'each word is one way of acknowledging Being' (*J.* 129), these notes allow that the function of recognizing and reciprocating God's stress, which is as we have seen so important to Hopkins, can be achieved directly through language: 'I did say yes | O at lightning and lashed rod' (*P.* 28, st. 2). The lecture notes on 'Rhetoric' develop this reciprocal relation by making spoken words themselves substantive, 'heavy bodies' that directly parallel objects of divine and human creation, 'objects of nature or man's art' (*J.* 269). Metrical stress is conceived of by analogy with ontological stress, an identification that Hopkins develops further through sprung rhythm. All of his poetry from 'The Wreck of the *Deutschland*' onwards was written to be read aloud and explores utterance as a way of acknowledging Being. The rest of this chapter is devoted to tracing the significance that the act of utterance has in this poetry.

Hopkins again renews the Pythagorean pun he made in 'Let me be to Thee' in an unfinished poem on the martyr Margaret Clitheroe, where he refers to the Trinity as 'The Immortals of the eternal ring, | The Utterer, Utterèd, Uttering' (*P.* 145). The 'eternal ring' is the unending line of the circle, but also the 'changeless note', which rings out forever in the Pythagorean music of the spoken word. It is the perfect circle of communication comprising the Father who utters, the Son who is uttered (that is, the Word made flesh), and the Holy Ghost, the perpetual act of 'Uttering'. This formula makes it clear that there is for Hopkins no distinction between the stress of divine utterance and ontological stress or grace. This equation between the spoken word and being can be traced back to Genesis, where God called the Creation into existence: 'And God said, "Let there be light"; and there was light' (Gen. 1: 3). Spoken words function in this biblical account as mathematics and music do in the Pythagorean cosmology – that is, as the source and structure of all order in the world. Divine utterance is, like the Creation, the Word or *Logos* made manifest and substantive, actualized: 'God's utterance of himself in himself is God the Word, outside himself is this world' (*S.* 129).

Hopkins's formula for the Trinity in 'Margaret Clitheroe' describes a God whose grace can be reciprocated in kind through the spoken word. It is through the Holy Ghost, the 'Uttering' itself, that we receive divine grace. But the Holy Ghost also operates *through* man (1 Cor. 12: 7–11), so that the act of 'Uttering' belongs to humankind not only as the form of divine grace we receive but as a way that we can respond to it. Hopkins develops his idea of the Holy Ghost as the 'Uttering' from his reading of the Bible. The name of the Holy Ghost, from the Greek *pneuma*, means, as Hopkins observes in a sermon 'on the Gospel John xvi 5–14':

> Spirit or Breath, for as the breath is drawn from the boundless air into the lungs and from the lungs again is breathed out and melts into the boundless air so the Spirit of God was poured out from the infinite God upon Christ's human nature and by Christ, who said: Receive the Holy Ghost: as my Father sent me so I send you/, was breathed into his Apostles and by degrees into the millions of his Church, till the new heavens and new earth will at last be filled with it. (*S.* 98)

The way in which this spirit is breathed into the Church, into the brethren, is through speech. Breathing and speech are used synonymously in a passage from John (20: 22) that Hopkins borrows from directly in his sermon (and which I have italicized): '*When Christ breathed on his disciples, saying/ Receive the Holy Ghost*, when the Bishop says the same over the priest he is ordaining . . . it is the Holy Ghost that is then given' (*S.* 99). Similarly in Genesis the first man is described as coming into being both through God's speech (Gen. 1: 26) and as he is infused with breath (Gen. 2: 7).

For Hopkins every breath that we take comes from God, the original 'giver of breath' (*P.* 28, st. 1), the source of the stress or grace that sustains us. Respiration, our constant interaction with the 'fine flood' (*P.* 60, l. 51) of the air, makes us very much like the fountain of the unfinished poem: 'Thee, God, I come from, to thee go, | All dáy long I like fountain flow' (*P.* 155). Breath, like the circulating blood it feeds, is one of the great gushing flushing flows of our physical being. While we necessarily spend our lives drawing upon God's gift of breath, we can give it back as utterance. Indeed, Hopkins describes the writing of his poetry in such terms, as a dedicated breath sent back to its source:

> This air, which, by life's law,
> My lung must draw and draw
> Now but to breathe its praise.
>
> (*P.* 60, ll. 13–15)

This reciprocating gesture of breath is demonstrated most simply at the close of 'God's Grandeur', where the Holy Ghost is identified with the freshness of the morning that the poet breathes in:

> Oh, morning, at the brown brink eastward, springs –
> Because the Holy Ghost over the bent
> World broods with warm breast and with ah! bright wings.

The apprehension of this fresh dawn draws from the poet an involuntary exclamation: 'ah!' All utterance is exhalation, but this aspirate 'ah!' is a deeper and purer release of breath than most spoken words, burdened as they are with their specific meanings. It marks the expiration of a deep refreshing breath, the grace of the Holy Ghost, which infuses the poet's being here as it does all nature, for 'There lives the dearest freshness deep down things' (*P.* 31). This 'ah!' is a 'counter stress' to the stress of divine grace, an 'aspiration in answer to his inspiration' (*S.* 158). In a letter to his mother from 1871 Hopkins describes the way that each of the two gardeners at Stonyhurst say 'Ay': 'He makes a kind of Etna of assent, without effort but with a long fervent breathing out of all the breath there is in him.' Indeed their prolonged expiration of the word, which 'runs through the whole scale of the vowels', leads Hopkins to 'believe it is a natural sign of agreement and not conventional' (*L3* 114). He understands such purely expressive aspirate sounds to be a natural gesture of assent. They occur at many points in Hopkins's poetry, as, for instance, in the sestet of 'The Windhover', where the 'fire which breaks from' the bird draws from the poet an 'oh', an 'O', and an 'ah' (*P.* 36). Indeed, such sounds are one of the defining gestures of his poetry.

It is precisely our counter-stress of saying or breath that in 'The Leaden Echo and the Golden Echo' constitutes the Golden Echo:

> Resign them, sign them, seal them, send them, motion them
>   with breath,
> And with sighs soaring, soaring síghs, deliver
> Them.
>
> (*P.* 59)

We can give back the treasures of mortal beauty 'early now, long before death' through prayer, by giving our word to God, both in the sense of pledging them, that is, to 'sign them', as in the signing of a promissory note or a will, and more radically still as utterance, to 'motion them with breath, | And with sighs soaring, soaring síghs'. Sighs are long, deep inhalations and then exhalations of breath that express resignation, the resigning of mortal beauty that is recommended here. We are also urged to 'sign' our breath in the sense of giving it direction, to point it towards God, as 'sighs soaring'. These 'sighs', which echo and instance the directional 'sign', are aspirational, 'soaring' heavenward. Like the hurling heart at the close of 'Hurrahing in Harvest', they aspire towards union with God. Indeed, in the notes 'On Personality, Grace and Free Will' Hopkins writes that 'the wish to correspond [to God's grace] . . . this least sigh of desire, this one aspiration, is the life and spirit of man'. Prayer can be accordingly understood in these terms as 'this sigh or aspiration or stirring of the spirit towards God'. He explains that the 'sigh or aspiration' of prayer or other such gestures towards God 'is a *forestall* of the thing to be done' (*S.* 155), which is to say that it is not the action itself but its anticipation. It is the *form* of the action and a pledge to action, as we 'sign them, seal them, send them, motion them with breath'. This central passage in 'The Golden Echo' draws us in as participants, so that in reading it aloud we enact this 'motion' of breath as a forestall of the prayer described here, which is itself a forestall of the act itself, the actual surrendering of our mortal beauty, of our being, to God.

All of Hopkins's poetry demands of us an enhanced and dedicated gesture of expiration: 'but take breath and read it with the ears, as I always wish to be read' (*L1* 79). Hopkins means his poetry to be given as much breath as possible, to be read 'loud' and unhurried, dwelling upon its rhymes and stresses: 'remember what applies to all my verse, that it is, as living art should be, made for performance and that its performance is not reading with the eye but loud leisurely, poetical (not rhetorical) recitation, with long rests, long dwells on the rhyme and other marked syllables, and so on' (*L1* 246). Indeed, 'Stress is the life of it' (*L1* 52), for metrical stress requires the most decisive, intense, and prolonged releases of breath. In a suggestive parallel to God's creation of man (Gen. 2: 7), metrical stress requires us to breathe life into what the lecture notes on 'Rhetoric' describe as the 'bodies' of words, and his doctrine of sprung rhythm specifies as the unit of the metrical foot. We breathe life into the dead matter of written ciphers: 'Sprung rhythm gives back to poetry its true soul and self.' Indeed, poetry is for Hopkins the Golden Echo of speech. Just as the Golden Echo is purged of the leaden dross of sin, so analogously 'poetry is emphatically speech, speech purged of dross like gold in the furnace' and sprung rhythm intensifies this further, 'it purges it [i.e. verse] to an emphasis as much brighter, livelier, more lustrous than the regular but commonplace emphasis of common rhythm as poetry in general is brighter than common speech'.[2]

As 'The Golden Echo' serves to highlight, the giving of breath in utterance is a gesture towards giving back to God our entire being, the soul that was originally breathed into us. Hopkins's poetry is accordingly like prayer, a *'forestall'* of this ultimate counter-stress of divine stress, the difference being that in poetry Hopkins is able through such means as sprung rhythm to intensify this gesture of utterance. The trinity of 'The Utterer, Utteréd, Uttering' requires a response in which the whole stress of being is focused in the act of utterance that is offered to it. This is why Hopkins is so insistent that his poetry is written to be read aloud. Whereas reading silently to oneself occurs in the mind and is relatively passive, utterance is active and bodily. Hopkins's understanding of generic man in 'Ribblesdale' as 'Earth's . . . tongue' is not rhetorical, it does not simply mean that man is nature's mouthpiece. Rather it should be understood literally, for the tongue is for Hopkins, like the 'limbs' in the 'kingfishers' poem, a mode of moral action, it is one of 'the features of men's faces' that physically 'plays' to God. This is made clear in 'The Wreck of the *Deutschland*', which, as the first poem Hopkins wrote after entering the priesthood, functions in part as an apology for writing poetry and a manifesto for the new type of poetry it introduces:

> Is out with it! Oh,
> We lash with the best or worst
> Word last! How a lush-kept plush-capped sloe
> Will, mouthed to flesh-burst,
> Gush! – flush the man, the being with it, sour or sweet,
> Brim, in a flash, full! – Hither then, last or first,
> To hero of Calvary, Christ's feet–
> Never ask if meaning it, wanting it, warned of it–men go.
>
> (*P.* 28, st. 8)

In this stanza the tongue is brought forward in all its vigorous physicality, lashing out its words like a crack of the whip, and crushing fruit in the manner of the 'strenuous tongue' in Keats's 'Ode to Melancholy', which 'Can burst Joy's grape against his palate fine'. Hopkins refers in a later poem to his personal sense of self as a taste: 'Bitter would have me taste: my taste was me' (*P.* 67). We came across this imagery earlier, in the passage cited in Chapter 1, where he writes that his sense of self is 'more distinctive than the taste of ale or alum, more distinctive than the smell of walnutleaf or camphor'. Indeed it is so distinctive as to be 'incommunicable by any means to another man' (*S.* 123). It can in other words be metaphorically sensed, tasted, by the tongue, but not directly expressed by it. In stanza 8 of 'The Wreck', however, that which the tongue hurls out is individual being itself, which is decisively expressed by its attitude to Christ. Spoken language here is definitive, 'the best or worst word' is a clear and final expression of personal identity, but it is also presented as liquid, as something that 'We lash' or pour forth. It accordingly suggests the root meaning of the word 'express', which is to press or squeeze out as an essence of selfhood, like the 'ooze of oil | Crushed' that 'gathers to a greatness', 'the grandeur of God' in 'God's Grandeur' (*P.* 31). The pouring-out of breath in the 'lash' of the word – 'Is out with it!' – is the release of the soul itself. The definitive expression, the 'last' word, of selfhood is poured out, ultimately in an act of *kenosis*, an emptying-out of the self, as this individual word is replaced with the Word itself, God or the *Logos*. God's being transfuses the being of the converted, 'flush[es] the man, the being with it'. The action of the 'lash', like that of a whip, breaks the integrity of the 'lush-kept plush-capped sloe', so that it is 'flesh-burst', an analogy to the man whose being will 'Gush! – flush' with the new life of Christ in a 'flash' that answers to and supplements our original expressive 'lash'.

God is introduced as 'giver of breath' at the start of 'The Wreck of the *Deutschland*' (*P.* 28, st. 1) – that is, at the very beginning of his new practice of poetry, which is distinguished by its gestures of reciprocating this gift of breath through utterance. This understanding of utterance is clarified in stanza 8 of the poem as a '*forestall*' of *kenosis*, a gesture of emptying the self. It is well exemplified by the stanza's thematic sound, the consonantal digraph 'sh', which demands of us an extended expiration that is often further lengthened by the stress on the vowel that precedes it: 'How a lúsh-kept, plúsh-capped slóe'. Such expiration also anticipates the last breath, the expiration of life itself:

> But man – we, scaffold of score brittle bones;
> Who breathe, from groundlong babyhood to hoary
> Age gasp; whose breath is our *memento mori* –
>
> (*P.* 75)

But this final expiration is, as the 'Heraclitean Fire' sonnet makes clear, something to look forward to as the prelude to resurrection. The carbon dioxide of the last breath is itself a form of 'ash', which through the Resurrection is revivified as the fresh breath of the Spirit, just as in 'God's Grandeur' the Holy Ghost renews the freshness of the earth and its air each morning, cleansing it of the residual pollution of human activities (*P.* 31). Similarly, in 'The Blessed Virgin compared with the Air we Breathe' human beings can through grace overcome sin and so triumph over death: 'Men here may draw like breath | More Christ and baffle death' (*P.* 60, l. 66–7).

'The Wreck of the *Deutschland*' celebrates an utterance that is not a '*forestall*', but the actual and complete giving-back of breath to the 'giver of breath'. The heroic tall nun 'lash[es] with the best . . . | Word last', and expires uttering 'O Christ, Christ, come quickly' (*P.* 28, st. 24). Hopkins appeals to God for inspiration to understand these last words:

> The majesty! what did she mean?
> Breathe, arch and original Breath.
> Is it love in her of the being as her lover had been?
> Breathe, body of lovely Death.
>
> (*P.* 28, st. 25)

The meaning of the nun's words, which is her embrace of a Christlike death, becomes apparent here in the rhyme of 'Breath' with 'Death'. The tall nun has so instressed Christ as to offer her whole being to him in death. Such utterance is at the heart of Hopkins's relation to God, and it is this that both reconciles his work as a poet to his religious vocation and gives his poetry such confidence and conviction:

> I did say yes
> O at lightning and lashed rod;
> Thou heardst me truer than tongue confess
> Thy terror, O Christ, O God.
>
> (*P* 28, st. 2)

In writing poetry Hopkins follows the doctrine of 'The Golden Echo' by dedicating its individual beauty to God, returning it to 'beauty's giver', for, as he writes to Dixon in June 1878, 'The only just judge, the only just literary critic, is Christ, who prizes, is proud of, and admires, more than any man, more than the receiver himself can, the gifts of his own making' (*L2* 8).

8

Hopkins and Other People

A journal entry for November 1874 records a walk that Hopkins took with one of his Jesuit colleagues: 'Walking with Wm Splaine we saw a vast multitude of starlings making an unspeakable jangle . . . Splaine wanted a gun: then "there it would rain meat" he said. I thought they must be full of enthusiasm and delight hearing their cries and stirring and cheering one another' (*J.* 261). It is not surprising that Hopkins felt he needed to be by himself for his reveries over nature: 'I saw the inscape though freshly, as if my eye were still growing, though with a companion the eye and ear are for the most part shut and instress cannot come' (*J.* 228). The preceding chapters of this study have focused upon Hopkins alone, tracing the independent development of his thought and poetry. This chapter and the next discuss some poems that move out from his private experiences and concerns to discuss ordinary people and his relations to them. As we have seen, several of his poems refer to human beings abstractly, in the manner of 'As kingfishers catch fire', as types of Christ. There are, however, a few in which Hopkins discusses not this transcendent ideal type for humanity, but what he classifies as specific types within society, such as the industrial and the rural worker, the respective subjects of a pair of poems from September 1887, 'Tom's Garland' (*P.* 70) and 'Harry Ploughman' (*P.* 71).

In a letter to Bridges explaining 'Tom's Garland' Hopkins outlines the ideological framework of the poem, the classical doctrine that:

> the commonwealth or well ordered human society is like one man; a body with many members and each its function; some higher, some lower, but all honourable, from the honour which belongs to

> the whole. The head is the sovereign, who has no superior but God and from heaven receives his or her authority: we must then imagine this head as bare (see St. Paul much on this) and covered, so to say, only with the sun and stars, of which the crown is a symbol, which is an ornament but not a covering; it has an enormous hat or skull cap, the vault of heaven. The foot is the daylabourer, and this is armed with hobnail boots, because it has to wear and be worn by the ground. (*L1* 272–3)

Just as the head can be seen surrounded by the dome of the sky, so, according to the doctrine of the divine right of kings that Hopkins endorses in his letter, heaven rallies round the Head, the sovereign, investing it with divine authority: 'Country is honour enough in all us – lordly head, | With heaven's lights high hung round, or, mother-ground' (*P.* 70). The golden crown symbolizes the celestial order that rounds and includes, embraces, the head of the sovereign. Conversely, the labourer in Hopkins's poem gains his identity in relation not to the heavens but to the ground. The title of 'Tom's Garland' refers to the row of steel nails around the sole of his boots. Hopkins's poem presents a basically feudal order, a social hierarchy that makes no mention of the middle classes, the modern capitalist and professional classes, who dominated and defined Victorian society. The sovereign and the rest of the ruling class are at the top and beneath them a huge lower class of labourers, which Hopkins represents in the protagonists of 'Tom's Garland' and 'Harry Ploughman'. Both are identified with the 'mother ground'. Harry Ploughman is, as we will see later, a part of nature, an organic growth from this ground akin to a tree. 'Tom Navvy' (*P.* 70), on the other hand, is at war with it, 'armed with hobnail boots . . . to wear and be worn by the ground' (*L1* 273).

Hopkins mentions to Bridges that he wrote 'Tom's Garland' with some satiric intent, but, unsure about the extent to which he realized it in the poem, observes apologetically that 'It has a kind of rollic at all events' (*L1* 266). He was evidently not entirely comfortable with his subject matter or sure about how to approach it. 'Tom's Garland' is, as Hopkins says, 'a very pregnant sonnet' (*L1* 274), full of suggestive symbols and images that disclose ambivalent attitudes to industrial labourers and their plight. The apparently ironical conceit of

'Tom's Garland', its coronation of the working man, is not developed satirically in the poem to contest or criticize the established social order. If anything the joke is on Tom, who is 'garlanded with squat and surly steel', the adjective 'surly' suggesting the mock majesty of arrogance. The status quo is, as may be expected from Hopkins's belief in the sovereign's divine right to rule, largely defended and justified by the poem. Parallel to the symbolic order of 'The Leaden and the Golden Echo', 'rare gold' is in 'Tom's Garland' naturally valued above such other metals as 'bold steel'.

The power and glory enjoyed by the ruling class are, according to the poem, warranted by their burden of care, while, conversely, freedom from such care is the privilege of the working class, who do not have such power or wealth. The poem outlines this rationale in its discussion of the unemployed, the 'Undenizened' who have no place in the hierarchy, and enjoy neither of the advantages that belong respectively to the ruling and the working classes. The unemployed are, as the poem puts it, 'beyond bound | Of earth's glory, earth's ease'. Hopkins's letter to Bridges elaborates upon this observation: 'this is all very well for those who are in, however low in, the Commonwealth and share in any way the Common weal; but that the curse of our times is that many do not share it, that they are outcasts from it and have neither security nor splendour; that they share care with the high and obscurity with the low, but wealth or comfort with neither' (*L1* 273–4).

This concern with wealth distribution and class was for Hopkins an abiding one. In another letter to Bridges, written in August 1871, it is the employed rather than the unemployed labourers who have his sympathies for not being allowed their just share of wealth and comfort:

> Horrible to say, in a manner I am a Communist. Their ideal bating some things is nobler than that professed by any secular statesman I know of (I must own I live in bat-light and shoot at a venture). Besides it is just. – I do not mean the means of getting to it are. But it is a dreadful thing for the greatest and most necessary part of a very rich nation to live a hard life without dignity, knowledge, comforts, delight, or hopes in the midst of plenty – which plenty they make. They profess that they do not care what they wreck and burn, the old civilisation and order must be destroyed. This is a

> dreadful look out but what has the old civilisation done for them? As it at present stands in England it is itself in great measure founded on wrecking. But they got none of the spoils, they came in for nothing but harm from it then and thereafter. England has grown hugely wealthy but this wealth has not reached the working classes; I expect it has made their condition worse. (*L1* 27–8)

Bridges did not answer this letter, which led Hopkins to conclude that his friend was 'disgusted with the *red* opinions it expressed' (*L1* 29). Here, as in so much of his work, Hopkins's independence of thought leads him to break with conventional ideas held by his peers. The letter to Bridges shows the roots of his compassion in 'Tom's Garland' for the plight of the working man and the unemployed, as well as his anxiety, which the poem also airs, about the ultimate consequences of the injustices they are subject to: 'I must tell you I am always thinking of the Communist future ... I am afraid some great revolution is not far off'. (*L1* 27)

Hopkins acquired much experience ministering to working-class people in such parishes as Liverpool, Glasgow, and the industrial town of Bedford Leigh near Manchester. If 'Tom's Garland' is a record of such experience, then he evidently found labourers to be a homogeneous group:

> Tom Heart-at-ease, Tom Navvy: he is all for his meal
> Sure, 's bed now. Low be it: lustily he his low lot (feel
> That ne'er need hunger, Tom; Tom seldom sick,
> Seldomer heartsore; that treads through, prickproof, thick
> Thousands of thorns, thoughts) swings though ...

Tom is robust in health, hearty in his appetites, psychologically uncomplicated and emotionally untroubled. He approaches 'his low lot' with vigour and cheerfulness, 'lustily'. 'Tom Navvy', like 'Harry Ploughman' with his similarly generic name, is clearly meant to represent a type. But, whereas in metaphysics and science the idea of types in nature, as, for instance, species, may be defensible, applying this idea definitively to groups of people within human society produces only stereotypes. Hopkins identifies the ruling classes in this poem with 'mind', while the working classes are described summarily with the contrasting principle of 'mainstrength'. It is understandable that Hopkins should identify with the former principle over the latter, given his slight physical stature, intellectual nature, and the broad class allegiances of his birth and education. Nevertheless, 'Tom's Garland' represents a change in attitude from the time Hopkins wrote his 1871 'communist' letter to Bridges, for he writes of the worker here not as exploited and suffering but as enviably content with his lot. This perspective may well have been determined by Hopkins's early years in Dublin. The experiences he had of the mind's torments during this time, some of which are documented in the sonnets of desolation, allow us to understand his justification for ruling-class privilege as more than an empty or opportunistic rationalization: 'O the mind, mind has mountains; cliffs of fall | Frightfall, sheer, no-man-fathomed' (*P*. 65). The 'mind' is in 'Tom's Garland' made of 'Thousands of thorns, thoughts': it is not a golden garland but a crown of thorns. The day-labourer, as ever identified with his boots, 'treads through, prickproof, thick' these thorns. Such insensitivity has a sort of glamour for Hopkins in 'Tom's Garland', as a complete freedom from the cares of the mind that torment him. But he also, as we know from 'God's Grandeur', identifies it with brutality: 'nor can foot feel, being shod' (*P*. 31).

'Tom's Garland' refers ambiguously to 'mother-ground | That mammocks, mighty foot'. The word 'mammocks' is a verb meaning to break up, shred, or fragment. The rather indecisive syntax and the pivotal position of the verb here allow it to refer to both the ground and the foot, yielding a sense that Hopkins glosses in his explanatory letter to Bridges that the foot 'has to wear and be worn by the ground'. But it is clear from the letter that once shod in hobnailed boots it is the 'mighty foot' that inflicts all the damage: this is, he writes, 'symbolical; for it is navvies or daylabourers who, on the great scale or in gangs and millions, mainly trench, tunnel, blast, and in others ways disfigure, "mammock" the earth and, on a small scale, singly, and superficially stamp it with their footprints' (*L1* 273). 'As it at present stands in England', Hopkins writes in the early 'communist' letter cited earlier, 'it is itself in great measure founded on wrecking' (*L1* 28). The labourer, identified synecdochically with hob-nailed boots, is the instrument of this national practice of 'wrecking'. In 'The Wreck of the *Deutschland*' Hopkins suggests that modern

England is founded on the wrecking of its Catholic Church, while in 'God's Grandeur' the wrecking of nature incrementally by such individual action as 'Tom's Garland' also describes is understood in religious terms as a desecration:

> Generations have trod, have trod, have trod;
> And all is seared with trade; bleared, smeared with toil;
> And wears man's smudge and shares man's smell: the soil
> Is bare now, nor can foot feel, being shod.
>
> (*P.* 31)

While 'Tom's Garland' allows us to look back to 'God's Grandeur' and read its remorselessly trodding 'Generations' as working-class hoards, this comparison reciprocally suggests that Tom and his fellow bootboys are sinners who 'lustily' infect the purity of nature with the smear, 'smudge', and 'smell' of their sweat and 'toil'. The lack of care that the labourer enjoys can be understood accordingly as an ignorant lack of feeling that allows him to brutalize the earth.

In an ironic parallel to 'heaven's lights', the sun and other stars that the sovereign's golden garland symbolizes, the garland of nails in the workmen's boots 'rips out rockfire', it produces sparks as the steel strikes the hard surfaces of the road home. As Hopkins puts it in his letter to Bridges, the workers 'swing off home, knocking sparks out of mother earth not now by labour and of choice but by the mere footing, being strongshod and making no hardship of hardness, taking all easy' (*L1* 273). This interesting image recalls such nature poetry as 'The Windhover' and 'As kingfishers catch fire', where the potential energy of stress is actualized, released, as fire. Whereas we can imagine the sovereign's golden garland 'catch[ing] fire' from the sun's light, rather as 'daylight's dauphin' does in 'The Windhover', and so connecting symbolically with the heavenly realm from which it gains its authority, the sparks produced carelessly and randomly by the steel garland of Tom's boots suggest a latent violence, the possibility that the 'mainstrength' of the labourer could find dangerous outlets outside work. Sparks are incendiary, each could be the agent of a huge explosion or conflagration. This sense of menace and foreboding was felt by many of Hopkins's social class during 1887, when large numbers of working and unemployed people chose to mark Victoria's jubilee with riots, strikes, and socialist mass rallies. In a poem that, as Hopkins's commentary makes clear, proceeds from the logic of its symbols, the image of the sparking hobnails anticipates the final lines of the poem, which describe what happens to labourers like Tom and his fellows when they are exiled from the workplace by unemployment. The synecdoche of the hobnails characterizes the workers through a crude version of Hopkins's ontology, his economy of stress or energy. Akin to other creatures, such as those of the 'kingfishers' poem, the labourer needs to express and so actualize his being. The natural and fulfilling expression of this vigorous physical stress is seen here to be organized work. Deprived of such work, the labourer's energy of being becomes baulked, either turned in upon itself in despair and depression, or 'worse' still turned outwards upon others in anger:

> This, by Despair, bred Hangdog dull; by Rage,
> Manwolf, worse; and their packs infest the age.

Just as the dull steel nails of 'Tom's Garland' can produce sparks, so from the despairing domesticated 'Hangdog dull' can come the red rage of the wild dog, the wolf. The 'Hangdog' is a base person fit only to be hanged like a dog, while the suggestion here is that the 'packs' of 'Manwol[ves]' also need to be controlled or destroyed, for they too describe 'pests of society' (*L1* 274). In the figure of the 'Manwolf' the brutality that 'mammocks', tears into, the earth now sets its sights on other human beings. Like the sparks from the dull nails, the violence of the 'Manwolf' suggests an analogous breaking-out of brightness, as flesh is broken and releases red blood.

The labourer's work is seen as brutal and destructive, his needs and satisfactions as simple and physical. He is a type, a subspecies of mankind who can degenerate into the predatory 'Manwolf'. The employed and the unemployed labourer are effectively characterized here as Dr Jekyll and Mr Hyde. Hopkins read Stevenson's *Dr Jekyll and Mr Hyde* soon after its publication in 1886, the year before he wrote 'Tom's Garland', and he was hugely impressed by it, describing parts of it as 'worthy of Shakespeare' (*L1* 238). While throughout his writings Hopkins follows an optimistic Aristotelian ontology, in which good and beautiful potential natures become actualized in actions and appearances, in Stevenson's novel he found the dark side of this principle explored as a gloss on human nature. Given Hopkins's sensitivity to the destruction of nature in such poems as 'God's Grandeur' and 'Binsey Poplars', it is not surprising to find him characterizing the labourer through his dictum '*What I do is me*' (*P*. 57) as brutal and dangerous. The 'Manwolf' is a bestial man like Stevenson's Hyde. The 'Hangdog' and the 'Manwolf' represent a potential for anti-social and revolutionary activities that, the poem suggests, lurks within contemporary working-class men and is realized when their energies are not constructively employed in labouring jobs: 'And this state of things, I say, is the origin of Loafers, Tramps, Cornerboys, Roughs, Socialists and other pests of society' (*L1*. 274). The poem suggests Hopkins's anxiety that 'bold steel' could usurp 'rare gold', the brutishness of 'Tom's Garland' could, through violent revolution, or indeed democratic means, replace the monarch's golden garland. The protagonist of 'Harry Ploughman', however, offers no such threat, as he represents a more reliable, ancient and natural, partner in the feudal order presupposed in 'Tom's Garland'.

Hopkins writes to Bridges that his intention in 'Harry Ploughman' was to produce 'a direct picture of a ploughman, without afterthought' (*L1* 262) – that is, without reflecting upon it. He may well have been thinking of his poem, which is devoted to a detailed description of the ploughman's appearance, by analogy to photography. He writes a few months after the poem was written that he was 'getting knowledgable in this matter, being amongst people who photograph' and that he distinguishes photography proper from its reworkings by 'painting, stippling, "touching"' as 'the lens-work and ... what that gives' (*L3* 290–1). This ideal of an unmediated or 'direct picture', which is in any case a dubious description of photography, is certainly not guaranteed in Hopkins's poem by its lack of 'afterthought', the fact that he does not self-consciously rework or interpret the image that was before him. Inevitably he has to make choices as to how to represent the ploughman, and the poem reveals the presuppositions that inform his choices here, which are all the more interesting for being fundamental and unquestioned.

From its title we might expect of 'Harry Ploughman' a Wordsworthian romanticism that champions rural workers and the rural poor. However, it is not the sensibility of the individual but the physical power of the man that is celebrated here. Harry Ploughman is summed up as an adjunct to the plough he guides: 'He leans to it, Harry bends, look. Back, elbow, and liquid waist|In him, all quail to the wallowing o' the plough.' The octave of the poem brings a machine aesthetic to its survey of the ploughman's body, which is described in obsessive detail as a powerful assemblage of muscle and sinew:

> Hard as hurdle arms, with a broth of goldish flue
> Breathed round; the rack of ribs; the scooped flank; lank
> Rope-over thigh; knee-nave; and barrelled shank –
>   Head and foot, shoulder and shank –
> By a grey eye's heed steered well, one crew, fall to;
> Stand at stress. Each limb's barrowy brawn, his thew
> That onewhere curded, onewhere sucked or sank –
>   Soared ór sánk – ,
> Though as a beechbole firm, finds his, as at a rollcall, rank
> And features, in flesh, what deed he each must do –
>   His sinew service-where do.

The ploughman's arms are each likened in their hardness to a 'hurdle', a bar of iron or wood, he has muscles like ropes crossing over the thighs, the knee is a 'nave' or hub of a wheel, and the calf muscles bulge in the cylindrical form of barrels. These mechanic parts of his muscular body work together like a ship's crew. The association that generates this image becomes clear when we look back to the sailors in 'The Wreck of the *Deutschland*' and 'The Loss of the *Eurydice*', which are similarly defined by their muscularity. The most specific depictions are the dead sailors, the one in the former poem with 'all his dreadnought breast and braids of thew' (*P*. 28, st. 16), and the one in the latter 'all of lovely manly mould' (*P*. 41, l. 74), a body that was shaped and defined by the physical demands of his job; 'he | Is strung by duty, is strained to beauty' (*P*. 41, ll. 77–8). The words 'strung' and 'strained' here speak of muscular exertion and development. In 'Harry Ploughman', the ploughman's muscles set to work as such a crew, they 'fall to'. They are mobilized like a crew at 'a rollcall' (itself a metaphor for the poem's catalogue of them) to 'Stand at stress'.

The descriptions of the sailor's and the ploughman's bodies as 'strung', 'strained', and 'at stress' indicate a mechanistic understanding of the muscles.[1] One of Hopkins's poetic fragments, 'To his Watch', parallels the human heart to a wristwatch:

> Mortal my mate, bearing my rock-a-heart
> Warm beat with cold beat company, shall I
> Earlier or you fail at our force . . .
>
> (*P.* 153)

The muscle that pumps the blood around the body is clearly understood here as a mechanism, as it shares with the watch the same mechanical 'force'. In 'Harry Ploughman' the coordinated movement of the muscles is similarly summed up by Hopkins's mechanistic ontology of 'stress', so that they are like the movements of the creatures in the octave of the 'kingfishers' poem, which are described by analogy with the mechanistic causal relations of inorganic nature, 'As tumbled over rim in roundy wells | Stones ring; like each tucked string tells . . .' (*P.* 57). The ploughman's 'grey eye', the ship's Watch, reflexively steers the 'crew' of muscles. Similar to the protagonist of 'Tom's Garland', but more directly analogous to the creatures in the octave of the 'kingfishers' poem, Harry Ploughman is presented as a type, a representative of a species, rather than a free-willed individual. He is an assemblage of muscles 'at stress', part of a mechanistic conception of nature that not so much parallels him to the plough as makes him inseparable from it, so that they form a primitive cyborg, the composite 'Ploughman'.

Just as Harry Ploughman's being is conflated with the machine he works with, so similarly the identity of the young sailors whose death is memorialized in 'The Loss of the *Eurydice*' is presented as inextricable from the matter of their ship. The Royal Navy frigate *Eurydice* was built in the 1840s and refitted as a training ship in 1877. The fatal storm that wrecked the ship in March 1878 and killed all but two of its 300 crew is summed up at the start of the poem: 'One stroke | Felled and furled them, the hearts of oak!' (*P*. 41, ll. 5–6). The sailors have become like the masts of the ship, trees 'Felled'. They are described as the substance of the ship itself, for such English warships as the *Eurydice* were, as the ninth edition of the *Encyclopaedia Brittanica* records, made from 'heart of oak', the strongest part of the timber, 'hard, close-grained, and little liable to split accidentally'.[2] It is, therefore, not so easy clearly to distinguish the tree of the ship from the flower of youth that was its crew: 'Must it, worst weather, | Blast bole and bloom together?' (ll. 15–16). The identification of the young men with the oak turns on their shared strength, or, more particularly, the muscularity by which they are 'strained to beauty'. Hopkins describes the oak as muscular in his early journals: 'Oak roots are silvery, smooth, solid and muscular' (*J*. 67). Another entry describes a wood of tall oak trees, their 'boughs spare . . . and gracefully and muscularly waved' (*J*. 146). Similarly in 'Harry Ploughman', 'Each limb's barrowy brawn', which largely sums up the ploughman in the poem, is likened not only to barrows, small hills or mounds of earth, but to the trunk of a tree, for it is 'as a beechbole firm' (*P*. 71).

9

Bodies and Beauty

The peculiar documentary objectification of Harry Ploughman, as the poem catalogues the details of his physical appearance, draws him into mechanistic nature rather than full humanity. In the sestet, however, the effort at objective description, 'a direct picture', of the ploughman's body softens with its extended description of his hair in the wind, 'his wind-lilylocks-laced', and the ascription to him of a masculine beauty or 'Churlsgrace' (*P.* 71). The sailors from the *Eurydice*, 'the hearts of oak' (*P.* 41, l. 6), are similarly identified with nature, and the poem is also attentive to their physical appearance. By transforming its human objects into objects of nature, the gaze itself need not be understood as 'unnatural' – that is, as anything other than sexually innocent. The representative type for the young sailors who died (*P.* 41, l. 85), the body 'of lovely manly mould', is introduced as having been witnessed by others, whose report the poet depends upon here (*P.* 41, l. 73). But this well-proportioned body is soon made the object of the poet's gaze and offered to that of the reader: 'Look, foot to forelock, how all things suit!' (*P.* 41, l. 77). It is an index of the taboo on male homosexuality, marked in Victorian times and necessarily all the more so within the priesthood, that the poet allows himself 'Look' admiringly at the 'lovely manly mould' only when, as 'one sea-corpse cold' (*P.* 41, l. 73), it is disqualified by death from being considered a sexually attractive object.

In a letter to Bridges in 1879 Hopkins writes: 'I think then no one can admire beauty of the body more than I do, and it is of course a comfort to find beauty in a friend or a friend in beauty. But this kind of beauty is dangerous' (*L1* 95). Such beauty is described similarly in the 1885 poem 'To what serves Mortal Beauty?':

> To what serves mortal beauty – | dangerous; does set danc-
> ing blood – the O-seal-that-so | feature, flung prouder form . . .
>
> (*P.* 62)

The rather unkempt interpolation within this first sentence of the poem itself suggests that the dangerous dancing blood can erupt at any time. Dancing, the courtship ritual that by degrees both facilitates and disciplines a couple's bodily movements together, is here used as a metaphor for the mild sexual pathology of increased heart rate, palpitations, and the like. The ultimate danger is mortal sin, but the dance of the blood here signals only the threat of this possibility. It suggests a danger of the kind that Hopkins refers to in his early confessional notebook: 'Physical danger while having my arm in Baillie's and speaking affectionately' (*PM* 196).

Mortal beauty preoccupies and disturbs Hopkins in a number of poems. 'The Leaden and the Golden Echo', as we saw earlier, urges us to avoid its anguish and despair by pledging it early to God. The bugler in 'The Bugler's First Communion', who is described as 'Breathing bloom of a chastity in mansex fine' (*P.* 48), appears to have made such a pledge, but the poem is nonetheless preoccupied with the vulnerability to mortal sin that his youth and looks give him. The poet-priest offers an oddly voluptuous image in this poem to describe the youth who comply with his message of chaste Christianity; 'limber liquid youth, that to all I teach | Yields tender as a pushed peach'. With its implications of physical ripeness and readiness for consumption, this sounds like a metaphor for seduction from a French libertine novel. But here, of course, it is meant to describe young adulthood morally ripe for, and receptive to, the priest's message. It is a troubled image.

'To what serves Mortal Beauty?' asks much the same question as 'The Leaden Echo' about the possibility of preserving physical beauty. '[T]he O-seal-that-so feature' describes the imperative wish to preserve the beautiful feature hermetically, as in a jar with a rubber O-ring seal clamped shut. This would also contain the danger that such beauty represents to itself and others, the threat to moral purity that the poet is so anxious about in 'The Bugler's First Communion'. But Hopkins does not see mortal beauty in itself as the problem here. Rather he looks to the viewer's response to it, which can take the form of either 'gaze' or 'glance'. The voyeuristic 'gaze out of countenance' (*P.* 62) not only embarrasses its object, it is also dangerous, for, as the undergraduate Hopkins notes, 'the attraction of some sins is greater the greater the attention of the mind' (*J.* 81). It is this that is likely to 'set danc- | ing blood'. The objectification of mortal beauty as purely physical threatens to prevail in 'Harry Ploughman' and 'The Loss of the *Eurydice*'. It is only after his body has been subjected to the sustained scrutiny of the gaze that the ploughman is attributed with having a 'Churlsgrace'. Similarly, the patriotic 'duty' by which the dead sailor 'is strained to beauty' furnishes an uneasy rationale for the poem's interest in the proportions of his body and the gaze it subjects it to. The 'glance', however, intuits immediately the ontological and moral significance of mortal beauty in an epiphanic 'flash' of the sort described in 'God's Grandeur', for such beauty is immediately striking as a manifestation of the good soul: 'Self flashes off frame and face' (*P.* 62). The physical beauty that Hopkins describes in his letter to Bridges as the lowest type of beauty can accordingly be recognized as the expression of the highest, the 'beauty of character, the "handsome heart" ' (*L1* 95).

In the 'Mortal Beauty' sonnet the beautiful physical 'feature' defines and distinguishes the beauty of the individual. It is the expression of selfhood, which, as he declares in his 1880 poem 'Henry Purcell', Hopkins finds in the music of his favourite composer: 'It is the forgèd feature finds me; it is the rehearsal | Of own, of abrúpt sélf there so thrusts on, so throngs the ear' (*P.* 45). While such 'forgèd' features distinguish particular individuals, all belong to Christ, the product 'of faultless workmanship' (*S.* 36). The beauty of Christ is, as the 'kingfishers' sonnet explains, distributed in 'the features of men's faces' (*P.* 57). The individual 'feature' accordingly expresses Christ, the ideal beauty of being itself, the goodness of created nature, so that it

> keeps warm
> Men's wits to the things that are;|what good means . . .
> (*P.* 62)

The 'Mortal Beauty' poem demonstrates the virtue of the 'glance' with an example it draws from church history of some 'lovely lads' similar to the sailors from the *Eurydice*. These are a group of young English slaves from the late sixth century, who being offered for sale in a Roman market caught the eye of the future Pope Gregory. Because he understood their beauty as the outward expression of a morally good nature, Gregory sent Augustine to lead an evangelical mission to convert the British. Whereas the mortal beauty of Harry Ploughman is rendered a beauty of nature, so that he is effectively equated with the creatures in the octave of 'As kingfishers catch fire', 'To what serves Mortal Beauty?' comes to recognize such physical beauty as expressing the Christlike good character in the manner of the sestet of the 'kingfishers' poem, where Christ is 'Lovely in limbs, and lovely in eyes not his' (*P.* 57). In this understanding, mortal beauty is not 'dangerous', but a grace of God that accordingly requires acknowledgement: 'What do then? how meet beauty? Merely meet it; own,|Home at heart, heaven's sweet gift, then leave, let that alone' (*P.* 62).

In 'To what serves Mortal Beauty?' Hopkins seems to be trying to discipline his sexual attraction to others by repudiating the 'gaze' in favour of the 'glance'. The poem shows his effort to organize and integrate his sexuality with his emotional and intellectual passions and desires in the private cosmology that much of this book has been devoted to explicating, a systematic understanding of the world that he evidently lived through. Hopkins not only defuses the provocative power of 'Mortal Beauty' by regarding it as simply another God-given beauty of nature. He also, conversely, diffuses it throughout nature as the mortal beauty of Christ:

> I walk, I lift up, I lift up heart, eyes,
> Down all that glory in the heavens to glean our Saviour;
> And, éyes, heárt, what looks, what lips yet gave you a
> Rapturous love's greeting of realer, of rounder replies?

Hopkins grounds his faith in the Incarnation, and understands nature accordingly as the physical incarnation of God – that is, as the type of Christ: 'And the azurous hung hills are his world-wielding shoulder' (*P.* 38). This metaphor, suitably adjusted to a more modest scale, is familiar to us from 'Harry Ploughman', where the muscles of the ploughman's limbs are described as small hills or mounds, 'barrowy brawn'. Nature is seen by Hopkins through the physicality of the male body in which God became incarnate as Christ, a human body that is gendered but uniquely not towards a sexual end. Understood in this way, the figure of Christ probably does, as Isobel Armstrong suggests, provide Hopkins with an acceptable focus and release for his 'troubled homosexual passions'.[1]

Hopkins values Christ and nature for their sanctified corporeality, the purity of their physicality. This is precisely the quality that his poem 'At the Wedding March' sees marriage to bestow upon the bride and groom:

> God with honour hang your head,
> Groom, and grace you, bride, your bed
> With lissome scions, sweet scions,
> Out of hallowed bodies bred.
>
> (*P*. 52)

The marriage ceremony blesses and sacralizes the bride and groom, it makes of them 'hallowed bodies'. Parallel to this, nature is depicted in 'Hurrahing in Harvest' as the hallowed body of Christ. St Winefred's well provides an instance of this incarnation for Hopkins, as, Christlike, the saint's defiantly pure body was not only resurrected but assumed the eternal 'virgin freshness' (*P*. 139) of this spring that bears her name. In 'God's Grandeur' the Holy Ghost maintains the purity and 'freshness' of the body of nature by cleansing it of abject masculine physicality, the bodily fluids of labour that have been wiped over the earth so that it is 'bleared, smeared with toil; | And wears man's smudge and shares man's smell' (*P*. 31).

The unfinished ode 'Epithalamion' (*P*. 159) that Hopkins began to write for his brother Everard's wedding in 1888 is also devoted to picturing nature as fresh and masculine. The poem is introduced as the poet's fantasy, which we are invited to share: 'Hark, hearer, hear what I do; lend a thought now, make believe.' We are positioned by the poem as voyeurs, sheltered by a leafy bower in a wood 'That leans along the loins of hills', where without being seen we see a group of 'boys from the town | Bathing' in a pool. We then spy another person who also looks at the boys, our proxy, 'a listless stranger' who 'unseen | Sees the bevy of them', and then goes for a swim in 'a pool neighbouring'. The phrase 'heavenfallen freshness' with which the poem sums up the scene is, as Norman MacKenzie notes, mistranscribed by Hopkins in a copy of the lines as 'heavenfallen freshmen' (*PW* p. 491). In place of a marriage between a man and a woman the poem records an odd baptismal ritual in which the no longer 'listless stranger' consecrates a kinship with the boys bathing in the next pool: 'Flinty kindcold element let break across his limbs | Long. Where we leave him, froliclavish, while he looks about him, laughs, swims.' At this point the poem makes several attempts to draw this material into its 'sacred matter', the genre's staple concerns with the wedding day and the couple's experience, but breaks off after a few fragmentary lines.

Hopkins thought that 'every one should marry' (*L1* 193). Drenched in 'virgin freshness', the pastoral fantasy that stands in for the 'Epithalamion' sketches a chaste and fulfilling relation between fresh masculine nature and a 'listless stranger', a figure who suggests the Hopkins of the Dublin years who wrote 'To seem the stranger lies my lot' (*P.* 66). Nature, which for Hopkins follows the pattern of Christ's Incarnation, is one version of the holy marriage partner. Correspondingly the priest works to be like the high-priest Christ, a chaste and hallowed body. He has taken his vows and strives to be worthy of his Saviour, 'the true-love and the bridegroom of men's souls' (*S.* 35). Hopkins's relationship with Christ and the Creation is a marriage of hallowed bodies, to which he brings his hurling heart and vigorous utterances. Each is active and physical in its expressive gestures, as they greet each other, throw and catch, echo and chime with one another.

Hopkins enjoys a remarkably expansive relationship with Christ, in which, as we have seen, he can look to 'all that glory in the heavens' and find in it 'looks' and 'lips' that give 'a | Rapturous love's greeting of realer, of rounder replies' than all others. These lines suggest Man Ray's painting *A l'heure de l'observatoire – Les amoureux*, in which a pair of inviting red lips traverse a summer sky. Hopkins's version of nature is surreal in its anthropomorphism, the way in which his understanding of it as incarnation allows him to collapse qualities of Christ with those of nature. In 'Hurrahing in Harvest', for instance, his Saviour's 'world-wielding shoulder | Majestic' is 'very-violet-sweet!', an identification that sensuously fills the mystery of Christ's perfect physical being with the intense colour and scent of the tiny flower, much as he does in a journal entry on a bluebell: 'I do not think I have ever seen anything more beautiful than the bluebell I have been looking at. I know the beauty of our Lord by it' (*J.* 199). Hopkins distils incarnate matter into sensuous values, the loving round 'looks' and 'lips' or the flowers' qualities, essences that he identifies with ultimate reality, Christ's being.

This fusion of sensuous values with an ultimate underlying form is nicely instanced in music and elaborated in Hopkins's Pythagoreanism. In 'Henry Purcell' the 'fórged feature' is a distinctive piece of music that expresses the selfhood of the composer and through it discloses human nature, for, as Hopkins declares in the dedication to his poem, Purcell has *'uttered in notes the very make and species of man as created both in him and in all men generally'* (*P.* 45). This statement recalls the musical analogy that Hopkins draws in 'The Probable Future of Metaphysics' of 'type or species' to 'the roots of chords' (*J.* 120). It is based in the Pythagorean presupposition that music can represent the nature of ultimate reality. However, music is for Hopkins not only mathematical form, but passionate and dynamic experience. The 'fórged feature . . . | . . .so thrusts on, so throngs the ear' (*P.* 45). This dynamism and passion belong also to the beautiful physical 'feature' in 'To what serves Mortal Beauty?':

> To what serves mortal beauty – | dangerous; does set danc-
> ing blood – the O-seal-that-so | feature, flung prouder form
> Than Purcell tune lets tread to? | See: it does this: keeps warm
> Men's wits to the things that are; | what good means . . .
>
> (*P.* 62)

These opening lines of the poem allow a more subtle and definitive understanding of the physical relationship that Hopkins feels able to have with incarnate beauty than the rather panicky response that the poem goes on to develop, which restricts involvement with it to the 'glance' of acknowledgement: 'then leave, let that alone'. Rather remarkably, having used the trope of dancing to describe the vicious danger of physical beauty, he proceeds immediately, in the same line, to use this metaphor to explain its inherent virtue. The form of the distinctive beautiful 'feature' is likened to a dance of such vigour and majesty that it exceeds that which the stately music of Purcell allows. The 'tread' here suggests a courtly dance while the dangerously dancing blood is presumably closer to the more unruly contact sport of folk dancing.[2] The beauty of the human 'feature' not only surpasses the greatest forms of art, instanced here by Purcell's music, but is likened to such art brought to life in dance, the translation of music into bodily movement. It is a version of the principle outlined in the 'kingfishers' poem, where 'Christ plays in . . . | . . . the features of men's faces' (*P.* 57). The chaste form of the beautiful 'feature' is figured in the 'Mortal Beauty' sonnet as Pythagorean: the physical incarnation of music. Indeed, the figure of the dance is implicit in the opening lines of 'Let me be to Thee as the circling bird', which come into focus with the pun on the word 'rings' as both physical motion and musical sound, a pun that is initiated here and, as we have seen, returned to in later poems.

The beautiful 'feature' of 'Mortal Beauty' is for Hopkins none the less vigorous for being chaste. It is not only a 'prouder' but a 'flung . . . form', like its type in Christ, who is 'heaven-flung' (*P.* 28, st. 34). It reminds us that 'The Handsome Heart' it expresses is not only decorously 'self-instressed' but 'wild' (*P.* 47). This dance is another of Hopkins's metaphors of reciprocal relation, akin to those of catching, greeting, and echoing discussed earlier. The 'flung . . . form' invites its partner, the person who recognizes its beauty, to 'meet' it appropriately in its dance. While this disqualifies the libidinous dancing blood, its impetuous movement requires a suitably impassioned response to match it, something more akin to 'a fling of the heart' (*P.* 28, st. 3) than a cursory 'glance'. 'Hurrahing in Harvest', in which the poet recognizes the incarnate beauty of Christ in all the features of the Creation, presents the ultimate and so most boldly delineated instance of this reciprocal action, as the heart 'hurls for him, O half hurls earth for him off under his feet' (*P.* 38).

The principle of form that Hopkins represents in the 'Mortal Beauty' sonnet with the dance is summed up in the last line of 'Henry Purcell' with the simple descriptive phrase 'meaning motion', which refers here not simply to Purcell's music but to the peculiar avian metaphors that the sestet uses to describe its genius and the poet's experience of it:

> Let him oh! with his air of angels then lift me, lay me! only I'll
> Have an eye to the sakes of him, quaint moonmarks, to his pelted
> plumage under
> Wings: so some great stormfowl, whenever he has walked his
> while
> The thunder-purple seabeach plumèd purple-of-thunder,
> If a wuthering of his palmy snow-pinions scatter a colossal smile
> Off him, but meaning motion fans fresh our wits with wonder.
>
> (*P.* 45)

In the first image the poet is lifted up by the music as if the composer were a great bird, so that he is able to see clearly his distinctive markings, the revelatory scapes, 'the sakes of him, quaint moonmarks'. Then, rather audaciously, this metaphoric large bird is itself likened to another large bird, 'some great stormfowl'. Hopkins makes it clear through his further analogy that his metaphor works reciprocally, so that each of its terms functions equally as a metaphor for the other. When the 'stormfowl' prepares to take flight, it also, just like Purcell's music, 'fans fresh our wits with wonder'. The phrase 'meaning motion' indicates that the stormfowl is intending motion, about to fly, but it resonates much more widely here, drawing in both the bird and Purcell's music as parallel instances of dynamic form. The 'meaning' of music comes through its 'motion', the relations of its successive parts in time, so that, for example, we describe the form of the symphony as a series of 'movements'. Similarly, in nature, the inscape of particular creatures comes through their distinctive activities, a kind of natural play or dance that articulates their meaning, their essential identity: *'What I do is me: for that I came'* (*P.* 57). Indeed, the stormfowl, a creature that belongs to all the elements of land, sea, and sky, suggests that the principle of 'meaning motion' she emblematizes characterizes the natural world in its entirety. This 'meaning motion' belongs reciprocally to our mind, the partner to the phenomenon itself, for it 'fans fresh our wits with wonder', a metaphor that recalls the imagery of 'The Windhover'. While the beautiful 'feature' 'keeps warm | Men's wits to the things that are' (*P*. 62), the experience of 'meaning motion' in nature, such as the stormfowl's flight, or the expressive humanity of Purcell's music, 'fans' the coals of 'our wits with wonder' so that they catch fire in epiphanic recognition of their full significance, much as the mind of the onlooker experiences 'the fire that breaks from' the Windhover as 'a billion|Times told lovelier' (*P*. 36) than the actual light reflected off the bird.

The 'meaning motion' at the close of 'Henry Purcell' recapitulates all the applications of Hopkins's principle of form, including the ontological inscape in nature and art, and the epistemological inscapes by which we come to know these things. But it is also implicit in the poetry itself: 'The thúnder-púrple séabeach, plúmèd púrple-of-thúnder'. The full, long and stressed vowels, the various 'u' sounds, give a richness and majesty that are appropriate to the purple colour, and a rumbling sound and thundering emphasis that lend verisimilitude to the synaesthetic description of the stormy seaside as 'thúnder-púrple'. The beach bears the reflection of the storm clouds, as does the bird's plumage, while the structure of the line, clarified by MacKenzie's restoration of the comma in the middle of it,[3] brings them into relation as mirror images of one another. This line demonstrates once again Hopkins's observation that his poetry contains 'excellences higher than clearness at a first reading' (*L1* 54). These excellencies spring from the meaning itself being enacted through the apparently obscuring word sounds. Rather than treating words as transparent windows to the things they signify, so that they yield 'clearness at a first reading', Hopkins brings to the fore their physicality, qualities that make them like 'heavy bodies' (*J*. 269). Meaning is thoroughly incarnate in language here, in the patterned motion of its sound sequences that make it a form of music. Its higher 'excellences' are those of the dance, of sounds that are bodied forth, given breath, and performed as physical acts of reading out loud. His poetry has the 'flung' quality of the dance in its systemic, vigorous orality, the intense tongue-exercising patterns of the word sounds and the accentuated exhalations demanded by sprung rhythm; 'Gush! – flush the man, the being with it, sour or sweet' (*P*. 28, st. 8). Like the two birds and the composer's spirit in 'Henry Purcell', Hopkins's poetry is born aloft on airs, the breath of utterance. He conceives of poetry accordingly as an art natural to humankind that shapes God-given breath, our fundamental 'fountain flow' of being, into forms that gesture gracefully back to God. Its utterance incarnates breath in the stuff of words, a performance that reciprocates the dance or play of Christ in nature, word for Word.

Spoken words give Hopkins a physical relationship to the hallowed bodies of Christ and Creation, of God in the world. This conception of words is, however, presented most directly in the 1880 poem 'Felix Randal' (*P*. 53) in relation to another human being. The poem memorializes a farrier to whom Hopkins ministered as he was dying of pulmonary tuberculosis. The poet recalls that he had administered confession and absolution and read Holy Communion to the dying man: 'I had our sweet reprieve and ransom|Tendered to him.' More than simply being proffered or 'Tendered', the sacred words are physical gestures of tenderness here, the speaking 'tongue' is paralleled with bodily 'touch':

> This seeing the sick endears them to us, us too it endears.
> My tongue had taught thee comfort, touch had quenched thy tears,
> Thy tears that touched my heart, child, Felix, poor Felix Randal

The communion between the priest and the farrier that is so delicately rendered in the balancing phrases of these lines comes through suffering, tenderness and touch through the type of Christ's terrible Passion.

'Felix Randal' demonstrates that spoken language afforded Hopkins communion not only with Christ and the Creation, but also with other people. Criticizing one of Bridges' verse dramas, he describes a principle that 'is of the first importance both in oratory and drama' and also, we might add, in his own performative art of poetry: 'I sometimes call it *bidding*. I mean the art or virtue of saying everything right *to* or *at* the hearer, interesting him, holding him in the attitude of correspondent or addressed or at least concerned, making it everywhere an act of intercourse – and of discarding everything that does not bid, does not tell. I think one may gain much of this by practice' (*L1* 160). Bidding describes Hopkins's mannerism, the demands his poetry makes upon us to reciprocate its gestures: to breathe, sigh, gasp, speak, help him when he is lost for words (*P*. 28, st. 28), 'Look!,' 'Give beauty back', share his joy in nature, love and fear God, *participate*. He wants us to read his poetry with the 'ears, as if the paper were declaiming it at you'. He figures his poetry here endowed with an independent life that we actualize and reciprocate through the being we share with it, for, as he goes on to explain, 'Stress is the life of it' (*L1* 51–2).

Hopkins explains to Bridges that 'It is most difficult to combine this bidding, such a fugitive thing, with a monumental style' (*L1* 160). Following Wordsworth, who writes that he wishes 'to adopt the very language of men' for his poetry,[4] Hopkins repeatedly attacks 'the archaism of the language' (*L1* 218) he finds in contemporary poetry on the principle that, as he declares to Bridges, poetry should 'arise from, or be the elevation of, ordinary modern speech. For it seems to me that the poetical language of an age sh[oul]d be the current language heightened, to any degree heightened and unlike itself' (*L1* 89). With the twist at the end here to the modernist principle of 'making strange', of defamiliarizing the familiar, he marks out his characteristic tendency to intensify language effects. He also explains that sprung rhythm works to bring poetry closer to ordinary speech: 'Why do I employ sprung rhythm at all? Because it is the nearest to the rhythm of prose, that is the native and natural rhythm of speech' (*L1* 46). Hopkins finds the life of his poetry in the shared being of breath as it was shaped by his contemporaries in the ordinary language of the day. His vigorous and original participation within this community of spoken words warrants his playful description of himself as a 'pleasing modern author' (*L1* 284).

Notes

CHAPTER 1. ECCENTRICITY

1. Quoted in Norman White, *Hopkins: A Literary Biography* (Oxford: Clarendon Press, 1992), 384.
2. Gerald Roberts (ed.), *Gerard Manley Hopkins: The Critical Heritage* (London: Routledge & Kegan Paul, 1987), 78. The full text of these notes is included in not only the first but also the second and third editions of the *Poems*.
3. Extracts from these writers are reprinted in ibid.
4. W. H. Gardner, *Gerard Manley Hopkins: A Study of Poetic Idiosyncrasy in Relation to Poetic Tradition*, i (London: Secker & Warburg, 1944), p. vi.

CHAPTER 2. CONCENTRICITY

1. J. Hillis Miller, *The Disappearance of God: Five Nineteenth-Century Writers* (Cambridge, Mass.: Belknapp Press of Harvard University Press, 1963; repr. with new preface, 1975), 276.
2. Plato, *Republic* 616B–617E.
3. Tennyson, *In Memoriam*, lv, l. 15.
4. William Paley, *Natural Theology; or, Evidences of the Existence and Attributes of the Deity, Collected from the Appearances of Nature*, 13th edn. (London: J. Faulder, 1810), 456.
5. Novalis, *Schriften*, ed. J. Minor (Jena: Eugen Diederichs1923). v. 2, 179, fr. 21, cited in Martin Heidegger, *The Fundamental Concepts of Metaphysics: World, Finitude, Solitude*, trans. William McNeill and Nicholas Walker (Bloomington, Ind.: Indiana University Press, 1995), 5.

CHAPTER 3. WORDS AND THINGS

1. Hopkins's analogy probably derives from his reading of Ruskin, who writes, for instance, of 'the sacred chord of colour (blue, purple, and scarlet, with white and gold) as appointed in the tabernacle; this chord is the fixed base of all colouring with the workmen of every great age ...' (*Modern Painters*, vol. iv, pt. v, ch. 111, § 24; E. T. Cook and A. Wedderburn (eds), *The Works of John Ruskin* (London: George Allen, 1904, vi, 69).

CHAPTER 4. BEING

1. For Parmenides' poem and an excellent commentary on it, see G. S. Kirk, J. E. Raven, and M. Schofield, *The Presocratic Philosophers*, 2nd edn. (Cambridge: Cambridge University Press, 1983), 239–62.
2. Campion Hall, Oxford, Gerard Manley Hopkins Papers, MS Notebook B. I. See Daniel Brown, *Hopkins' Idealism: Philosophy, Physics, Poetry* (Oxford: Clarendon Press, 1997), chs. 7 and 8, for extracts from these notes (pp. 217–18) and a fuller discussion of their contexts and implications.
3. James Clerk Maxwell, 'Report on Tait's Lecture on Force: – B.A., 1876', in Lewis Campbell and William Garnett, *The Life of James Clerk Maxwell* (London: Macmillan, 1882), 648.
4. Gilles Deleuze and Felix Guattari, *A Thousand Plateaus: Capitalism and Schizophrenia*, trans. Brian Massumi (London: Athlone Press, 1988), 257–72.

CHAPTER 5. KNOWING

1. Norman H. MacKenzie, *A Reader's Guide to Gerard Manley Hopkins* (London: Thames & Hudson, 1981), 82–3.
2. Christ is the 'effulgence' (Heb. 1); Wisd. 7. 26.

CHAPTER 6. LIVING WITH GOD

1. Plato, *Republic* vii.
2. W. H. Gardner, *Gerard Manley Hopkins: A Study of Poetic Idiosyncrasy in Relation to Poetic Tradition*, i (London: Secker & Warburg, 1944), 150.

CHAPTER 7. BREATHING IN AND SPEAKING OUT

1. Letter to Everard Hopkins, 5 Nov. 1885, *Times Literary Supplement*, 8 Dec. 1972, 1511. This letter is also reprinted in *Hopkins Research Bulletin*, 4 (1973), 10.
2. Letter to Everard Hopkins, *TLS*, 1511.

CHAPTER 8. HOPKINS AND OTHER PEOPLE

1. This understanding was well established and widely accepted by the time that these poems were written. See e.g. Sir Charles Bell, *The Hand: Its Mechanism and Vital Endowments as Evincing Design*, Bridgewater Treatise 4 (London: William Pickering, 1833), especially 108–16, and *Encyclopaedia Brittanica*, 9th edn, i (Edinburgh: Adam & Charles Black, 1875), 834.
2. C. Pierpoint Johnson, 'Oak', in *Encyclopaedia Brittanica*, 9th edn, xvii (Edinburgh: Adam and Charles Black, 1884), 690, 691.

CHAPTER 9. BODIES AND BEAUTY

1. Isobel Armstrong, 'Hopkins: Agonistic Reactionary – the Grotesque as Conservative Form', in Armstrong, *Victorian Poetry: Poetry, Poetics and Politics* (London: Routledge, 1993), 433.
2. This 'tread' may also refer to the military march, which similarly choreographs the body's movements to music, albeit in a more disciplined and less tactile way than the dance.
3. The comma from MS B of the poem is introduced to the printed text in MacKenzie's 1990 edition. See *PW*, p. 404.
4. 'Preface' to *Lyrical Ballads*, in *Wordsworth's Literary Criticism*, ed. W. J. B. Owen (London: Routledge & Kegan Paul, 1974), 74.

Select Bibliography

WORKS BY HOPKINS

The Letters of Gerard Manley Hopkins to Robert Bridges, ed. Claude Colleer Abbott, 2nd (rev.) impression (London: Oxford University Press, 1955). Hopkins has a fine prose style, and his letters are very readable and often amusing. His closest friend who later became the first editor of his poems, Bridges insisted upon being kept up to date with Hopkins's poetry and, finding it difficult, elicited from him in these letters many useful commentaries on individual poems and his poetic practice generally.

The Correspondence of Gerard Manley Hopkins and Richard Watson Dixon, ed. Claude Colleer Abbott, 2nd (rev.) impression (London: Oxford University Press, 1955). Canon Dixon taught Hopkins briefly at Highgate. He became a close correspondent from 1878 after Hopkins wrote to him admiring his poetry. This volume also includes letters that Hopkins contributed to the journal *Nature* on the remarkable sunsets that occurred after the eruption of the volcano on Krakatoa in 1883.

Further Letters of Gerard Manley Hopkins, ed. Claude Colleer Abbott, 2nd edn. (London: Oxford University Press, 1956). This volume includes letters to his family, including a series on his conversion, and correspondence with several of his friends from Highgate and Oxford and with his fellow poet Coventry Patmore.

The Journals and Papers of Gerard Manley Hopkins, ed. Humphry House and Graham Storey (London: Oxford University Press, 1959). This indispensible volume includes Hopkins's early diaries and journals (which contain his exacting and lyrical nature observations, notes on language, drafts of early poems, and records of his social and religious life until 1875), and many very fine reproductions of his early Ruskinian drawings. The volume publishes some of the more important of his early Oxford essays on philosophy and his Birmingham notes on words and on Parmenides, in which he introduces his terms 'stress', 'instress', and 'inscape', along with his notes for his Roehampton lectures on Rhetoric, in which he outlines his theory of poetry and verse.

The Sermons and Devotional Writings of Gerard Manley Hopkins, ed. Christopher Devlin (London: Oxford University Press, 1959). A fascinating complement to the *Journals and Papers*, this volume contains Hopkins's extant sermons and private spiritual writings. In particular, his extensive private notes on the Ignatian Exercises develop and deepen his early philosophical speculations, and offer important ideas and contexts for reading the mature poetry.

The Poems of Gerard Manley Hopkins, ed. W. H. Gardner and N. H. MacKenzie, 4th (rev.) edn. (Oxford: Oxford University Press, 1970). A widely available, comprehensive, and scholarly edition, which judiciously incorporates and develops the work of the earlier editors, Robert Bridges and Charles Williams, as well as Gardner's third edition. It features useful notes on the poems and translations of Hopkins's Greek and Welsh poems.

Journals and Papers of Gerard Manley Hopkins, ed. Giuseppe Castorina (Bari: Adriatica, 1974). Includes the first publication of some school notes on classics and two Oxford essays, one on scientific method, the other on sculpture.

Gerard Manley Hopkins, ed. Catherine Phillips, The Oxford Authors (Oxford: Oxford University Press, 1986). Authoritative texts of the poems in chronological order, with selections from the prose, and scholarly notes.

The Early Poetic Manuscripts and Note-books of Gerard Manley Hopkins in Facsimile, ed. Norman H. MacKenzie (New York: Garland, 1989). This is notable for being the first publication of Hopkins's early confessional notebook. Leaving aside the editor's often rather quirky essays, the facsimiles of the poems and other writings make this volume and *The Later Poetic Manuscripts* listed below useful reference works.

The Poetical Works of Gerard Manley Hopkins, ed. Norman H. MacKenzie (Oxford: Clarendon Press, 1990). The definitive edition thus far of Hopkins's poetry, with all works, both complete and unfinished, arranged together in chronological order and furnished with detailed textual and explanatory notes.

The Later Poetic Manuscripts and Note-books of Gerard Manley Hopkins in Facsimile, ed. Norman H. MacKenzie (New York: Garland, 1991).

BIOGRAPHY

Martin, Robert Bernard, *Gerard Manley Hopkins: A Very Private Life* (London: Harper Collins, 1991). By focusing upon the private person, and seeing his conflicted sexuality as a key to his life and work, this enlightening work draws upon new sources to offer a critique of traditional approaches to the poet.

White, Norman, *Hopkins: A Literary Biography* (Oxford: Clarendon Press, 1992). A thorough and comprehensive contextual biography of the poet.

CRITICAL AND SCHOLARLY WORKS

Armstrong, Isobel, 'Hopkins: Agonistic Reactionary – the Grotesque as Conservative Form', in Armstrong, *Victorian Poetry: Poetry, Poetics and Politics* (London: Routledge, 1993), 420–39. This elegant essay succinctly identifies the interweaving political, metaphysical, and sexual dynamics that register and wrestle in Hopkins's distinctive and 'decadent' poetic style.

Beer, Gillian, 'Helmholtz, Tyndall, Gerard Manley Hopkins: Leaps of the Prepared Imagination', in Beer, *Open Fields: Science in Cultural Encounter* (Oxford: Clarendon Press, 1996), 242–72. This exemplary historicist reading charts Hopkins's independent speculative engagements with contemporary physics, principally acoustics and optics, and the cosmologies they facilitated.

Bristow, Joseph, ' "Churlsgrace": Gerard Manley Hopkins and the Working-Class Male Body', *English Literary History*, 59 (1992), 693–711. This provocative essay places Hopkins's representations of Christ's physicality and potency in the context of the late-Victorian middle-class homoerotic interest in muscular working-class men, and argues that his mature poetry evidences his troubled efforts to establish a distinctively masculine poetic.

Brown, Daniel, *Hopkins' Idealism: Philosophy, Physics, Poetry* (Oxford: Clarendon Press, 1997). Drawing extensively upon Hopkins's largely unpublished and hitherto neglected early essays and notes on philosophy, this study argues that contemporary British Idealist thought and energy physics were decisive for the development of his distinctive thought and poetry.

Cotter, James Finn, *Inscape: The Christology and Poetry of Gerard Manley Hopkins* (Pittsburgh: University of Pittsburgh Press, 1972). A very useful book, which through close reading of the poetry and much of the prose relates Hopkins's religious experience and belief to primary sources in Christian theology.

Ellsberg, Margaret R., *Created to Praise: The Language of Gerard Manley Hopkins* (New York: Oxford University Press, 1987). Explores the development and implications of Hopkins's sacramental ideal of language. In doing so it furnishes a clearly written, good introductory study of the poet.

Fennell, Francis L., *Rereading Hopkins: Selected New Essays* (Victoria, Canada: University of Victoria, 1996). A diverse group of essays, of varying quality, which discuss Hopkins in relation to his Vedic influences, Jewish mysticism, Ricoeur's hermeneutics, Reception Theory, Poetics, and issues of gender and sexuality.

Gardner, W. H., *Gerard Manley Hopkins: A Study of Poetic Idiosyncrasy in Relation to Poetic Tradition*, 2 vols. (London: Secker & Warburg, 1944, 1949; reissued Oxford University Press, 1958). A historically important work, which offers a comprehensive introduction to Hopkins's innovations in prosody and interesting comparisons with other canonical poets.

Hartman, Geoffrey, *Hopkins: A Collection of Critical Essays* (Englewood Cliffs, NJ: Prentice Hall, 1966). Includes important essays by Hillis Miller (an edited version of the essay from *The Disappearance of God*, see below), Hartman (revised for this collection), and Marshal McLuhan.

Heuser, Alan, *The Shaping Vision of Gerard Manley Hopkins* (London: Oxford University Press, 1958). This is still a very good scholarly introduction to Hopkins's writings, which manages in a little more than 100 pages clearly and comprehensively to trace the growth of his thought and poetry.

Hopkins Quarterly. The journal of Hopkins Studies.

MacKenzie, Norman H., *A Reader's Guide to Gerard Manley Hopkins* (London: Thames and Hudson, 1981). Separate commentaries on each of the poems, which follows the sequence of the fourth edition. Offers useful explanations and contexts for understanding the poems, as well as some interpretations.

Miller, J. Hillis, *The Disappearance of God: Five Nineteenth-Century Writers* (Cambridge, Mass.: Belknapp Press of Harvard University Press, 1963; repr. with new preface, 1975), 270–359. A very enlightening discussion of how Hopkins understood and dealt with the Victorian crisis of belief, the apparent withdrawal of God from the world.

—— 'Hopkins', in Miller, *The Linguistic Moment: From Wordsworth to Stevens* (Princeton: Princeton University Press, 1985), 229–66. A most impressive and stimulating essay, which locates Hopkins's self-consciousness about language and poetry, and the theological and existential ambitions he has for them, in the contexts of European Romantic thought.

Milroy, James, *The Language of Gerard Manley Hopkins* (London: André Deutsch, 1977). A methodical and comprehensive discussion of Hopkins's linguistic registers and innovations, based on a close reading of the texts. Includes a useful reference section, which explains Hopkins's coinages and rare words that he adopts and adapts.

Plotkin, Cary H., *The Tenth Muse: Victorian Philology and the Genesis of the Poetic Language of Gerard Manley Hopkins* (Carbondale, Ill.: Southern Illinois University Press, 1989). A very useful and scholarly historical study.

Roberts, Gerald (ed.), *Gerard Manley Hopkins: The Critical Heritage* (London: Routledge & Kegan Paul, 1987). Collects early comments (1877–1918) and critical responses to Hopkins's work (1918–1940). A fascinating resource, which not only documents the early formation of Hopkins studies but still offers some fresh and suggestive approaches to the poet.

Sprinker, Michael, *'A Counterpoint of Dissonance': The Aesthetics and Poetry of Gerard Manley Hopkins* (Baltimore: Johns Hopkins University Press, 1980). This book establishes the apt and fruitful applications of structuralist and poststructuralist thought for Hopkins studies. It places the poet's ideas of language and self in relation to Victorian philology and the formalist aesthetics of Mallarmé, Russian Formalism, and American New Criticism.

Storey, Graham. *A Preface to Hopkins*, 2nd edn. (London: Longman, 1992). This introduction divides the contexts of Hopkins's work into his life, religion, and literary background, before offering readings of a number of his best-known poems. By one of the editors of the *Journals and Papers* (1959).

Sulloway, Alison, *Gerard Manley Hopkins and the Victorian Temper* (London: Routledge & Kegan Paul, 1972). Places Hopkins's work in relation to Oxford, Ruskin, Tractarianism, millenarianism, and the chivalric ethos of the Victorian gentleman.

Index